BANKERS,
HUG YOUR CUSTOMERS

BANKERS,

HUG YOUR CUSTOMERS

A GUIDE TO EVERY BANKER TO DELIGHT CUSTOMERS, EMPLOYEES, AND COLLEAGUES

SYED HUSSAIN

PARTRIDGE
A Penguin Random House Company

To order additional copies of this book, contact
Partridge India
000 800 10062 62
orders.india@partridgepublishing.com

www.partridgepublishing.com/india

CONTENTS

This book is dedicated to

The memory of my beloved parents
for teaching me human values,
My wife Asif, Nawab's daughter who came
to live with a humble man like me,
Mehnaaz (daughter) and Naser
(son) my pride and delight.

PREFACE

Everybody talks about customer service and it has been in sharp focus for the last so many years. But do we get good customer service anywhere including banks? Yes, we do get, but occasionally. In the post liberalization era after 1991 and of course with the entry of private and foreign banks, there is some improvement. The private and foreign banks initially impressed the customer with the introduction of speed of service and technology but in the long run failed to win their absolute trust. Public sector banks initially were under awe and shock from these entities and then took a leap stride in the introduction of technology. Particularly SBI, the largest commercial bank of the country not only outpaced the competitors in the introduction of technology but also won the trust of the customers.

Trust is the key variable in banking sector. Conservatism and proper assessment in identifying the needs and repaying capacity of the borrowers have helped public sector banks in retaining the trust of the customers. Many banks in the USA including the largest financial firm Lehman brothers collapsed due to improper assessment of the borrowers. In the words of Ms Beth Payne, US counsel- General to India "India has weathered the economic storm better than most because of its sound banking sector".

Once the customers repose their trust, it's imperative for the banks to reward them with excellent customer service. It is not surprising to see long queues in the banks even after the introduction of high end technology products like ATMs, internet banking and phone banking. The reason is economy still is cash based. It will take some more time for the Indian economy to move from cash to plastic money.

The rise in Indian economy has led to consumerism. Having got the luxury of different alternatives or choices of product and services— today's customer expects more and better services. Interestingly banks in India offer near identical products to the customers. Surveys and experience have shown that customers are deeply unhappy with service levels.

It is time now to move on to charismatic customer service to retain and improve customer loyalty. During my tenure as Branch Manager of eight branches in two states (A.P & W.B) I had many happy incidents of customer service. Experience itself is education and I felt the need to share with you how to hug customers to build customer loyalty and retention.

Fortunately the banks have an advantage over other corporate companies. Most of the bank branches are just like small stores. Each bank branch has on an average 5000 to 10000 customers. Pareto's principle says 80% of the business comes from 20% of the customers. Generally the Staff and the Manager know most of their customers personally and they have a broader idea of the customer's value and perception. Many of the staff members have close intimacy with frequent buyers of the services and products. Branches can afford to give time and attention to the customer and lay a foundation of excellent customer service.

The staff personally knows whether Mrs. Susan is a big depositor or a high ticket borrower. This will help the staff to give personalized service to their valuable customer. When it comes to customer service, we have no choice. We have to either improve it or lose the race of winning customers. Customer service is an art that takes time and effort to master.

The purpose of this book is to provide bankers the foundation to achieve great success in attracting, retaining and delighting the customers. I am not promising any amazing techniques here but simple and honest approach to win the customer for life. Dip in this book from time to time to recharge yourself in adopting some of the workable techniques of customer service. I am sure this book will stimulate you to hug your customers frequently and improve your business. A hugged customer will stay with you through thick and thin

ACKNOWLEDGEMENTS

I would like to thank all those colleagues who worked with me in branches and offices of the bank who influenced my ideas in writing this book. I would like to thank ex-Principal of State Bank Institute of Rural Development and the present Chief General Manager of Bhopal Circle Shri M.Bhagavant Rao for his exuberance and generosity in encouraging me in the initial stages of writing this book. He not only read a few manuscripts but also used his pen wherever necessary. I am highly indebted for his support and encouragement. My special thanks to Dr. K.R.S.Nair, Assistant General Manager and faculty of SBIRD using his surgical intervention and linguistic prowess to transform my manuscripts into something more readable than I could have accomplished on my own. I am especially grateful to Dr. B.A. Prabhakar Babu, Professor of phonetics, University of English and foreign languages and a long time friend for sparing his precious time to dust-off the flaws from the manuscripts. I immensely thank him, for his timely help. I was delighted when Mrs. Linda Prabhakar Babu, a geologist, told me that while reviewing the chapters he read some portions to her.

In addition, I want to thank my Vice Principal Shri.M.M Shaik, colleague faculties of SBIRD and particularly Smt.M.Jayshree Reddy, Assistant General Manager for her timely sixth sense advise. My immediate boss at Kolkata Mrs. Sibani Mallik, Assistant General Manager was a constant source of guidance, constructive feedback and support. I am grateful to the system Managers Mr.D.S.N.Murthy and M.Seshagiri for their assistance.

I thank Mrs. S.B.Singh Chief. Manager, Faculty SBLC Dehradun and Mr. K. Raghunandan, Assistant General Manager, SBIRD for graciously willing to help and filling the dents in the manuscripts. Mrs.S.B.Singh generous comments at the end of some of the manuscripts, she reviewed, kept me going. Some of her comments that touched my heart were "uproariously hilarious" and "hugely readable."

1

PASSION FOR HUGGING

What is hugging? Any simple pleasing gesture is called hugging. It could be as simple as a smile or greeting customer by name. If you want to stand out in the crowd, you have to repeatedly impress your competitors in many ways that your competitors do not. Every time you hug your customer you have improved your competitiveness in the market. To be ahead from the rest of the pack in marketing you have to develop strategies in winning and retaining the customer. Do little things better and do them often that customers notice like pulling a chair for the customer, walking with him to the exit door, offering a cup of tea and many such things.

Your name should stick in the customer's mind like a song that won't go away. Whenever a customer thinks about banking, your bank's image should strike his mind. Never in the history of banking has the need been greater for nurturing and creating strong relationships.

Passionless relationship

Incidentally my wife has got an account with a bank close to our home for the past fifteen years and never had she received any communication except a notice for non payment of locker rent. We all experience the same, passionless relationship from banks, hospitals, municipal office and school of our kids.

Hugging is to get closer to customer so that you become a friend and a confidante. Hugging should come from the bottom of heart; it should be real and sincere. When we are courteous, polite and well mannered with customers, they tell others. There is certainly a big payoff in being polite. Treat the customers the way you treat your parents, spouse, kids and friends. Take care of customers, they will come back and also bring their friends. We just don't want to deal with somebody just once but we want his business for ever. To create, sustain, and manage beneficial relationship, hugging the customer is indispensable. Hugging is a binding force between two parties.

When most customers are opting for electronic banking there are fewer opportunities for bankers and customers to interact. But if hugging is a passion in your functioning, customers will come to derive pleasure in doing business with you. They will personally visit your branch the way they visit a friend.

Hugging is team work

Hugging should be done at every level and frequently. Hugging at the branch is team work. Every employee should be geared to hug the customer. Hugging should begin as soon as the customer enters branch. Every employee of the branch should greet the customer with a smile; it starts from the watchman who stands at the entrance, the messenger in the banking hall, the front line staff, accountant and the manager. The strength of any organization lies in its employees and their attitude. Hugging should be embraced at all levels and it should be demonstrated with passion.

If a customer is hugged, he will ignore our mistakes. It is just like our savings bank account, hugging goes in credit and mistakes in debit. If customer is frequently hugged, credit increases in hugging saving account and a few mistakes will not create an overdraft. Generally customer ignores our mistake if it is not repeated. Loyal customers will be generally forgiving.

Non personalization

When the malls arrived in India many political parties took to the streets asking the government to ban their entry. It is now clear that they did not make much dent in the business of mom and pop stores (kirana stores). This is because of non-personalization. In the mall many items are not available. The staff is not properly trained, they have poor knowledge about the products and they fail to help the customers in locating the items. They neither greet us nor call us by name and there is no hugging. On the other hand our mom and pop store owner knows our buying habits; he does more hugging by smiling, calling us by name and enquiring about our kids. If some item is not available in his store he will source it for us. Research has shown us that personalization is a major factor in satisfying purchase experience. The more they delight the customers, more they come back for repeat purchase.

Parents taught us manners

In childhood it was our parents, who taught us to say,

- Please
- Thank you
- Sorry

We also teach our children the same three words "please, thank you and sorry". These are the most powerful words in the world which we frequently use. The entire world uses these words. These words never hurt anybody. Our customers if often told 'thanks' and 'please', will consider us highly mannered and cultured. Say 'sorry' if any mistake occurs. When you finish the customer transaction say 'thanks' for visiting the branch. If the voucher is incomplete, say, "please fill it". These small words will endear you to the customer. Interestingly when we took our son for admission to the nursery the teacher after the interview offered chocolates. Immediately he said 'thanks'. The teacher smiled and he was selected for admission. As a matter of fact they wanted to know about his upbringing.

Letter of thanks

One of the big hugs is the letter of thanks sent to customer for opening account with us and a letter of thanks to the introducer for introducing the customer. It is statutory and most of the times it is not sent and often pointed in branch inspection as irregularity. The customers and the introducer who received letter of thanks always expressed happiness. The first impression is the most powerful means of creating a lasting relationship.

Greeting the customer by name

Is one of the most powerful and disarming hugs. 'Nothing is sweeter than the person's own name". We all want to be addressed by our name. When someone calls us by name it brings us closer to the person and a warm sense of appreciation rings in our ear. It shows friendliness and makes us feel important. It improves customer retention, loyalty and business. Surprising it costs nothing to call a person by name and it helps to increase business. Employees should be encouraged to remember the names of the customers.

Reward and recognition

There should be a reward and recognition programme for remembering the maximum number of names. One should remember names of the top, at least 100 customers. If you remember more than 100 names surely you are a hugger. In my sessions as a faculty, I first ask the participants to introduce themselves. When they are speaking I look at their face without distraction and listen to what they say. I immediately repeat the person's name. This helps in getting pronunciation of the name correctly. Then during the session I call their names a few times. At the end of the session I call each one of them by his name and after the last participant is called they all spontaneously applaud. They often ask me to give the tips on remembering the names which I do cheerfully,

1. Carefully listen to the person without diverting your attention.
2. Make eye contact to concentrate on listening.
3. Repeat the person's name in his presence so that he can guide you to pronounce properly.
4. Repeat the customers' name many times during conversation.
5. Connect the person with his facial features, his extra ordinary height, his profession and slowly you will develop your own method of remembering.
6. Don't call a person by wrong name. It will be just like slapping. If you forget his name, recognize him first because he also knows that you will be meeting a lot of customers, so it is difficult to remember everyone by name. Instant recognition diffuses the situation. Coolly ask his name and repeat it several times. I bet you will never forget again.

Treat customer like a friend

Offer him a cup of coffee and have a friendly chat with him. Go into details about his family members their names, their occupations, his hobbies, and his nick name till you get very familiar with him. Ask his dog's name and remember it. On an informal friendly chat customers provide valuable information. Next time when they visit you can say" Hello Sam, how are Pinky and Randhir" his kids. The customer will be blown for your remembering his name and his children's names. Now he will be a friend and his loyalty will improve. He will find the bank more homely type rather than commercial or mechanical one. While ordering tea for customer, tell the tea boy to get tea with or without sugar because that was the tea last time he had taken. If some one doesn't drink tea, offer him coffee, thumps up, coca cola or any thing of his choice. These are simple things but they work wonders.

Greeting on birth day

I maintain a birth day diary in which the name, account number and phone numbers of the customer is written and it is frequently updated by employees. This diary is always with me for reference irrespective of my place of posting. First thing in the morning on reaching the branch I open the dairy and make call to the customers. I say "Good morning sir, Hussain from bank, happy birth day".

"Thanks, Hussain for the greeting". Then he sheepishly tells "actually it is my official birthday." I also humorously tell them "I am also officially conveying". This mostly happens with people who were born before 60's. But this is not so with our children whose birthdays are celebrated with a lot of fanfare.

To the customers who celebrate birthday this was something new to receive greetings from bank. On receiving our greetings early morning some of the customers visited our branch with a packet of sweets or a big cake and the entire staff greeted them and shared the sweets. But this was not making much impression with the older and valuable customers.

Marriage anniversaries

So I started conveying my greetings on their marriage anniversaries. I would call them and say "good morning sir, happy marriage anniversary". Now they cannot say it is official or unofficial. I would take permission to call their better half. I would say "good morning maam, happy marriage anniversary". These women consumers were surely delighted for the greeting. Women particularly never forget their marriage anniversary like men. By nature women have maternal instincts and they reciprocate my greeting by sending sweets and cakes to the branch. A simple greeting had connected our branch with the entire family.

Return –hug

A lady officer of our corporate client had applied for enhancement of her home loan. After completing the formalities we recommended for sanction of loan and dispatched the loan application to our RACPC. Unfortunately it was wrongly delivered by the courier. When the lady approached our RACPC they informed her that it was not received by them. The lady came to the branch, was annoyed and very furious. We showed her our dispatch register to convince her that it was promptly sent by us but she was not convinced. However the application was traced, the loan was sanctioned and it was disbursed. To iron out the unpleasantness I telephoned her to convey my greetings on her birthday. Ironically the call was received by her husband and he informed me that she was not at home. I requested him to convey my birthday greetings to her. After that I was transferred from that branch to another location. Since most of my customers have my mobile number they often contact me. When most of the people were queuing up to withdraw money from ATMS of a private bank, she in a panic telephoned me to know the procedure of transferring the money on line. I explained her patiently till she understood. I understand she felt guilty over what had happened earlier and reminded me of that particular incident. I told her, "at home sometimes brother and sister quarrel, then do we remember what they have told us". She was mighty pleased, thanked and hung up. As my daily routine of calling customers and greeting them, the following year I phoned her and again it was received by her husband. I asked for her. He immediately obliged me and she was on the line. I cheerfully greeted her "happy birthday ma-am". She was very pleased that a manager of the bank remembers her birthday even working at a different location. She felt immensely happy and invited me to her home. To my surprise the following year on 1st January she sent me a SMS greeting 'happy New Year'. When the customer feels happy and equally responds it is called a **return hug.**

Achievement greetings

Don't miss any opportunity to get connected to the customer. The secret to create customer loyalty is by sending greeting messages on their and their children's achievements. Loyalty of the customer could be achieved in a cost effective and friendly manner. The simple gesture of sending greetings will immensely impress the customer and create a long lasting relationship. Greeting cards are the best way of communicating with the customer. It will delight the customer and will also lead to referrals. So look out for their achievements and always convey it through greeting cards. Buy some greeting cards, keep it in your drawer and use it on appropriate occasions.

PROMOTION GREETINGS

I had amazing employees. They were the people who guided me and implemented my instructions wholeheartedly. Shri. Pasala Ravi, senior assistant of the branch once informed me that one of our corporate clients had promoted 149 of its employees in various categories. This was a big opportunity for us to hug. We categorized the customers on their designation and bought promotion greeting cards from 'archies' one of the leading greeting card companies. We obtained the list of promoted employees from their personal department. I and my staff visited each customer and delivered the cards. Before handing over the cards we read the beautiful words written in the card loudly to them. Generally greeting cards are accepted by people and not read, so we adopted this novel method of showing our gratitude to them.

Retirement cards

Visit the stationary shop and choose an appropriate card. The card should inspire and bless the retiree and not mock at him. You can also choose on the internet and send him through an email. This was a big hit with the retiring customers. In one of our staff meeting, how to retain the accounts of the retiring employees of our corporate client was discussed and a solution was worked out. Our accountant Smt. G.Annapurna, volunteered to obtain from their personnel department the list of retiring employees. The list helped us to plan our strategies. Most of these officials after retirement transferred their accounts and fixed deposits to the bank branch near by their home. These officials receive huge retirement benefits. A day before the retirement I used to call on the retiring officials accompanied by one of staff our member with a big beautiful retirement card. We used to stand before the customer, read the contents of the card and then hand it over to him. A month before retirement a meeting with the executive of SBI life insurance and SBI mutual funds was invariably arranged. This helped in winning the confidence, trust and friendship of the customer who continued to maintain his account with us, even after retirement.

Give your mobile number

Whenever a customer approached me, I did not give my visiting card but asked him to save my number on his mobile and also saved his number. Saving their number helped me in recognizing their call and responding by their name which made them instantly happy. It also helped me to send greetings on New Year, festivals, promotions and many such occasions through SMS. It also assured them that their bank manager was available to them any time, to listen and to help solve their problem. This was a big hit. Customers call me over mobile to seek my advice even now when they knew that I am not their branch manager.

Visit the customer in person

Always find time to call on the customer personally at his home. But be careful and choose proper time to call. It is better to take an appointment. The customer will be pleased to receive you at his residence. If they offer you tea, coffee, take it, don't refuse otherwise they will be offended. If alcohol is offered refuse it. At home they will feel free to discuss many personal things which may not be possible at the Bank branch. Your visit will pay big dividends because the entire family will come closer and consider you as their friend.

Receive the customer at the entrance

Manager should spend at least half an hour daily at the entrance and receive customers, the way people receive guests in marriage and other family related functions. Manager should frequently take a round of the banking hall during business hours. This will obviously help him to meet customers and instantly attend to their problems. Whenever you find old and infirm customers waiting for their turn to receive payment, immediately arrange cash and help them to get back in their cars or auto rickshaws.

Pension day

Every first of the month was an opportunity for the branch to hug our senior citizens. Pensioners need to be taken care of and made to feel special. Stripped off their titles they look with eager eyes to be recognized, respected and a craving to communicate. They invariably visit the bank on 1st to draw pension and meet their friends. Mr. R.Adam, senior assistant and Mr. N. Prabhakar, special assistant volunteered to report at the branch an hour earlier so that tokens were issued, their accounts debited, pass books updated and the moment cash was delivered at the counters it was promptly disbursed to them. We used to serve hot tea and biscuits to our esteemed senior citizens while some of our staff members engaged themselves in chatting with them and helping them to get in their vehicles. That day was always special for our branch and these customers were our ambassadors to spread the message of our service.

Encourage employees to call customers

Every week the employees should call customers, chat with them, take a feed back, and provide information to the manager. Interestingly when the customer herself directly tells the employee about the service, ambience, and time taken for delivery it will have a profound effect on the performance of the employee. The employees will feel empowered and take upon themselves to improve the service at the branch.

How often sellers contact us

We regularly bought grocery, clothes, electronic gadgets and books, but a couple of weeks later did any one of them call us to know how we liked their product? I would get carried away if any of them called me. I may express my opinion and I would certainly go to them for repeat purchase. Calling the customer and asking about the service or product after sale will create a bonding. Communicate with your customers regularly. This will obviously help us build relationships; customers will perceive that we have genuine concern and they will do more business with us and will refer us to their friends.

Bonding with a particular employee

Some customers have a bonding with a particular employee because of his hugging nature. In my branch Satish, a senior assistant was the most preferred employee of the customers. He was in charge of fixed deposit counter. In his absence most often customers left the branch without transacting the business. We also bond with a particular hair dresser, tailor, laundry boy who satisfies us. Sometimes I refuse to get my hair done with another hair dresser in the parlour. This is bonding which we all experience. Encourage employees to bond with the customers.

Technology hugs

It is important and it should be designed to meet customer needs, preferences and to make his life easier. Technology is a way of life in modern times and it should be designed to support hugging. My customer once narrated an incident when he left his house at 4 am in a taxi to the airport and suddenly noticed that he had no money in his purse. He panicked and asked the driver to stop at one of our bank ATMS and withdrew the cash. He felt immensely happy that at an unearthly hour he could get cash to meet the dire need of paying the taxi fare. This is technology hugging.

Consistence in hugging

The mantra of the winning team is consistency. The customer expects consistently excellent service all the times. It should be offered every time he comes in contact with us. The exceptional service shall be offered at every point right from payment of cash to pass book printing, receipt of cash to delivery of draft and for many such services at the bank. At any point of contact customer should not feel neglected.

Common courtesy

During lunch time don't just go for your grub. Always be courteous, provide tea and biscuits to the customers. This will make the customer realize that they bank with caring people. Keep chocolates and biscuits in your desk drawer and offer to the kids accompanying their parents.

Hugging colleagues

What do you do to make your colleagues feel special? Do you know their birth days, marriage anniversaries, and their kids' birthdays?

What have you done during the year to make them happy? When you create a hugging culture, every body should be taken care of. The way you treat your colleagues, the same way they will treat you and your customers.

Hugging ideas in nut shell;

1. Hugging should be embraced at all levels.
2. Send letter of thanks for account opening.
3. Greet the customer by his name.
4. Greet the customer on birthday, marriage anniversary, festivals and on many other happy occasions.
5. Provide your mobile number.

Hug, hug and hug your customer.

Hugging deficit

When we don't hug properly it creates a deficit in our relationship with the customer. The customer will be a fence-sitter ready to jump on the other side of the fence on the slightest opportunity. He has no attachment with us. He comes to us out of necessity for opening the account, withdraw money from the ATM, issue cheques, buy drafts and for many other services. Whenever he finds our competitor is giving more interest he will transfer his funds. He will invest in our competitor's mutual funds, insurance schemes and wealth management plans. There are many such faceless customers. Sometimes we had perceived these customers as small potatoes and not much of importance and never tried to hug them.

Many times on our visit to customers we have noticed the calendar of our competitor adorning their walls. Customer will also be singing praises of our competitors' service. This shows clearly that our competitor is ahead of us. Customers need more than a smile, sir or madam and greetings. There should be a proper, continuous communication channel with them.

Most customers rarely complain. They don't want to make a fuss. They simply walk away and never come back because we have failed to identify their problem. They were never heard, no feed back was obtained, and we assumed they always complained. No effort was made to hug.

Let the customer come to us, is the mindset. If there is a need the customer will come, why we go to him? Most of the Indians have inherent feudal mindset; they are yet to come out of their shell. They think that the customer may take advantage of friendliness. He may ask us to waive charges on draft, loan without security, may use our phone and may unnecessarily chat. It is better to keep distance from the customer. We have provided a rack stacked with vouchers so he can pick it from there. He can transact the business at the counters, use ATM to withdraw cash, we have provided internet banking and mobile banking which has many utilities. There is absolutely no necessity to meet the manager. But we think that some customers still come to the manager just to satisfy their ego. They disturb us; we already have much business to handle than to chat unnecessarily with these customers.

Going across the road

One of our bank branches was located in front of a medical college, hospital and in between the branches of two public sector banks. The manager was an efficient hard working person and when ever the doctors came to the branch he sanctioned housing loans, car loans and personal loans. The branch was in profit and the controller was happy that they have a very good manager. But most of the doctors banked with the other public sector bank. Our manager had never walked across the road because of his mindset that we serve whoever come to us. He missed the opportunity of attracting most of the doctors because he was shy to hug.

Tell me your name again: this shows that he is not an important person. This will further infuriate the customer who has approached you to complain. If you have forgotten his name it is preferable to say "sir" and then try to find his name from his pass book or by entering his account number on the screen.

You are the first person to complain about our service

Some managers react sharply about a complaint. They make the customer defensive and a trouble maker. It is always better to listen because there is every chance to improve our service. The matter should be discussed with the customer, and politely convey that our service is much appreciated by most of the customers. However your suggestion will help us to further improve it.

Try to be brief, I have to attend meeting

Customer is more important than any meeting. If you are really in a hurry, ask him to excuse you politely, take his cell number and assure him to contact. Once you have finished your work call him and discuss the matter. Otherwise entrust the job to the next person in command. Keep in touch with the customer. Let the customer feel he is a very important person.

Commit your team to perform hugging

2

CUSTOMER SERVICE

Customer service is the life line of any business. Prompt service not only makes a customer instantly happy but also persuades him to go back to that business and to spread positive feedback about it to others. This, in turn, makes the business more profitable. Good customer service simply builds relationships and the customer will be happy to continue such relationship, leading to a win-win model. The secret of delighting customer service lies in what you do and not what you say. Building excellent customer service skill of your employees is of utmost importance to the overall image of your bank and more particularly of your branch. The customers today are least loyal and would hop from one bank to another to take advantage of the freebee offerings product wise.

Definition of customer service: According to Jamier L Scot "Customer service is a series of activities designed to enhance the level of customer satisfaction – that is, the feeling a product or service has met the customer expectation".

But I will give a simple definition which you will find easy to remember "exceeding customer expectations". For example a customer comes to the branch expecting that his work will be done in 10 minutes but if he is attended and the work is completed in just five minutes, you have exceeded his expectation. This is good customer service.

Customer service is important because good customer service keeps the customers coming back. The ambience of the branch, the cheerfulness of the employees and their willingness to help immensely attract customers. Customers want proactive staff to solve their problem. Customers enjoy interacting with pleasing employees.

If you want to stand in the crowd, you should repeatedly impress your customers in many ways that your competitors do not. Do little things better and do them often that customers notice like pulling a chair for the customer, walking with him to the door to say good bye, offering a cup of tea and many such things.

Every time you have made your customer happy, you have improved your competitiveness in the market. Please remember customers expect fast, efficient and happy service.

It is important to acquire new customers but also vital to hold on to existing customers. Let us take a look on these statistics,

- Repeat customers spend 33% more than new customers
- Referrals among repeat customers are 107% greater than the new customers
- It costs 6% more to sell something to a prospect than to sell the same thing to an existing customer.

A study conducted by the federation of Independent business (NFIB) IN Washington D.C showed that small business which put heavy emphasis on customer service was more likely to survive and succeed than competitors who emphasized such advantages as lower price or type of product.

Losing a customer is expensive. According to the customer service institute, 65% of the company's business comes from existing customers, and it costs five times as much to attract a new customer than to keep a keep an existing customer. It costs as much to gain one new customer as to keep five existing ones. This clearly indicates that by maintaining good customer service you will be keeping customers – which in the long run are cheaper than finding new ones.

Highly satisfied customers

The Harvard business review reports that if you can prevent 5% of your customers leaving you, you can improve your bottom profit line by 25% to 95%. Eighty two percent of the lost clients go somewhere else because of a customer service issue.

The purpose of the business is to create and retain customer. Companies with high retention also grow faster. When customers are merely satisfied with the service they receive may walk away but highly satisfied customers will continue to do business with you and also recommend others.

- Happy customers tell 4-5 others of their positive experience.
- Dissatisfied customers tell 9-12 how bad it is.

The most important thing with the banks in offering better customer service is innovation in technology, products and services and if they ignore innovation they will be sowing the seed for self destruction. A customer expects from the bank customer service solid like "**ROCKS**",

R- Stands for reception, it means how the customer is received and greeted on entering the bank branch.

O- Organization, how the organization is effectively functioning in providing profit. C- Courtesy. The customer wants to be treated with courtesy at all levels.

K- knowledge, the customer wants to deal with knowledgeable employees who provide details of the products in convincing manner.

S- Service. The customer expects the service to be fast efficient, error free and to be delivered without hassles. The customer should be provided unexpected delights to demonstrate that she is highly valued and never ignored.

The key to achieve more profit is to deliver customer service beyond the expectation of the customer. The customer should feel relaxed and happy with your service constantly. The manager and staff should be focused, sensitive about the customers' needs and enhance the customer experience. The Manager should build, inspire and motivate his team to focus on customer loyalty, customer care, and customer retention to increase profits.

Great Customer service is perhaps the only thing that separates us from the rest of the pack as most of the banks offer similar products. Great customer service is critical to business. To achieve this it is important to inspire and motivate the employees to create a culture of excellent customer service. The employees should be impressed that the real benefit of excellent customer service is the good feeling that comes with making another person happy and the pride of doing a job well. The rewards are great because positive word of mouth will attract more customers. The most vital thing in customer service is to know how any customer wants to be served. For example in a predominantly employee based area the customer need is to have early business hours to transact the business before proceeding to their office, they would prefer a late closing branch in businesses dominated area. Quite often the bank believes they know the target area to sell their products but after spending time, money and energy they realize that what the customer need is something different. The need of a customer differs from area to area like recurring deposit in residential areas to insurance policies in office locations. If the banks fail to understand the specific want and need of a customer they will switch to their competitor.

Types of customers-- customers come with different flavors. They could be,

1. short tempered,	4. polite
2. patient,	5. systematic
3. lovable,	6. Complaining type

The short tempered customer spoils the atmosphere and leaves a very unpleasant day for the employee and the manager. Possibly he has hypertension and gets irritated often on the slightest sly. Most often he realizes his shortcomings and adjusts to the situation. But the complaining customer is a problematic customer. He finds fault with everything and anything. This type of customer has to be dealt with utmost patience and chivalry.

Say sorry-- when something goes wrong. A few days back I was flying with the national carrier not famous for its service but the behavior of individual employees makes a difference in the service. The plane was late by 2 hours, it was dinner time and like many other passengers I was also feeling very hungry. On my request an isle seat was allotted but against my wish it was in the middle of the plane. After take off the air hostess started serving the meal from the front end. She served the meal to the passengers in the front row and then turned to the left row opposite to my seat and by the time my turn came she had exhausted the food trays. I was upset and seized with anger as all the passengers in the plane were served food except me. She disappeared and after a few minutes appeared with a food tray. With the tray in the hand, she profusely said sorry for the delay and my anger disappeared for her sincere apologies. There was a sudden paradigm shift from anger to happiness and empathy for the employee because this was beyond her control. The situation of complaint of not serving food was diffused by her sincere apologies. I felt happy that the employee realized the need of the passenger and she was sincere in performing her duties. The five letter word "sorry" made a huge difference and had completely changed my emotions in a few seconds.

Learn and memorize words and phrases-- the employees and the supervisors should learn and memorize a few words, phrases that diffuse the tension to create an excellent customer service environment. They should learn and practice saying the phrases "oh, it is my fault", "sorry", "thanks". These are simple phrases and words that are going to make your angry customers happy. By saying "oh, it is my fault" the employee owns responsibility for the position and the customer feels relaxed as the mistake has been accepted. The employee can use the word "sorry" for any mistake committed during transaction because to err is human and accepting mistake is chivalry. The employees, the manager, the supervisor all should passionately use the word 'thanks'. This will give a message of acknowledging gratefulness to the customer.

Importance of language-- Speak the language which the customer understands. The story goes like this when the British, American and Japanese businessmen were asked in which language they would like to do business. The British and the Americans said they want to do business in English whereas Japanese said they would in customer's language. India has (22) Official languages and (1652) other languages. Every 100 kilometers the dialect differs. It is advisable for the banks to post personnel who can speak proficiently in the local language to effectively deal with the customers and gain their confidence. So, if you are doing business in an area where Bhojpuri/Munderi/Mythali/Bangru is spoken, then the employees fluent in that particular language should be posted as the customers will be more comfortable to speak in their language rather than any other language. This will fetch customer loyalty, referrals and repeat business. The employees should be encouraged by giving incentives to learn the local language as it is given for learning of foreign language.

Learning new language-- There is a beautiful story to narrate about an enterprising and innovative manager in learning a new language to delight the customers. In the late 1990s, an enterprising Starbucks store manager noticed that more and more deaf customers were frequenting her store. At first, this store used paper notes and awkward hand motions to communicate with these customers. But the store manager wanted to make these deaf customers feel more welcomed in her store. So she, and a handful of her staff, began learning sign language. By learning a different language to speak with these deaf customers, this Starbucks store became a hub for the local deaf community. Business, customer respect, and customer loyalty all got increased thanks to learning a different language the customer was speaking.

Handling an irate customer-- when a customer gets annoyed because of some lapse it is pretty difficult to handle because he is expressing his displeasure in his own style. It could be sudden outburst or body language because they are going through an emotional or stressful moments. The angry customer takes out his anger on the person they are talking to directly or over the phone. The need of the customer is to get the problem solved and he makes his problem as your problem. The **front line employees** are more **vulnerable** to such situations. Handling such customers needs training but it could be accomplished effectively if handled properly. Here are some of the best techniques to handle an irate customer.

1. **Stay calm**. The person who remains calm is in control of his emotions and operates from his position of strength. This will not further precipitate the problem and allow the customer to vent his feelings.
2. **Listen**. Never argue with the customer or arraign him as wrong. Nobody has ever won an argument with the customer. You listen carefully, and then in your own words, explain what you understood from what he said. The customer will feel relaxed if you have understood his problem or would clarify if your understanding was astray.

3. **Acknowledge**. If a mistake has occurred first acknowledge it. The customer will appreciate such a gesture. Nobody is infallible.
4. **Ask questions**. Such questions work as ice breakers. Ask relevant questions during narration of the problem by the customer so as to put him at ease and feel satisfied that you are paying attention and listening.
5. **Offer solution**. After listening to the customer, explain to him the way it will be rectified. The solution should be agreed upon by the customer and then only rectification should be done. If the customer is not happy with the proposed solution, provide him an alternative to his satisfaction.

Cultural sensitive care-- Banks preferably should post employees of the same cultural background in a given area. So, if you are doing business in an area with preponderance of minorities, then some of the front line employees, if not all, belonging to the same community should be posted. The customers will be more comfortable in dealing with them and repose more faith in them for transacting the business. They will exchange greetings in their own custom. The employees belonging to that particular community will serve as liaison to the Manager. There will not be any culture gap between the customer and the employee. When American troops invaded Iraq, every American soldier was provided with a copy of the customs of the Iraqi people. They were taught to greet, shake hand with right hand and not with the left, as the latter is used for performing not onerous jobs by the people of Iraq.

GREET THE CUSTOMER-- Greet them warmly, sincerely and genuinely. Always greet customers with a smile. Greet the customer with her name and keep on repeating the name during the conversation if the customer is known to you. Name is the sweetest thing a person wants to listen; it sounds music in his ears. Greeting the customer by name helps him feel that you care for him personally. If he is a first time customer, ask his name and repeat it so that he can correct your pronunciation of his name; and it will also serve as an exercise for you to remember his name. Greet also the other customer who is in proximity. If you don't remember his name, say "hello", or "nice to see you again". It shows you recognize him. A customer wants to be recognized immediately. When a customer is promptly greeted and recognized he will wait patiently for his transaction with a positive attitude. Customers like cordial and friendly environments. They will surely come back frequently to transact business with you.

Handshakes---- These are optional. When the customer is known to you extend your hand for a handshake. From behind the counter, a handshake may not be possible. Waiving the hand there is enough. Manager should always extend his hand for a firm handshake. But in Indian culture the ladies mostly do not shake hands. Don't extend your hand for hand shake with the ladies. My suggestion is to wait with both your hands at your side until the lady makes the first move. Needless to add, hugging, kissing and air kissing is strictly 'no'. Young college students and film personalities do such things, but surely it's not for the bank managers or bank employees.

Never meet the customer sitting-- The moment a customer enters your room, please stand up and receive the customer. Don't receive the customer while seated. There is a pretty story about mannerism to narrate. I was posted at Fort William branch of my bank as Branch Manager. Fort William is the Headquarters of the Indian Army Eastern Command headed by a Lt Gen. As a branch manager I am supposed to call on customers. I took an appointment from his adjutant to call on the Lt Gen. On that particular day, 15 minutes before the appointed time, I reached the Eastern Command Head Quarters. At sharp 11 a.m I was escorted to his room. The moment I entered the Lt Gen stood up with a warm smile and extended his hand for a firm handshake. I was amazed at the manner with which he received me. Lt Gen who commands more than 2 lakh troops had an inimitable courtesy to stand and receive his guest. He politely asked for my preference for a cup of tea, coffee and as per my choice tea was served.

I took the opportunity to explain our involvement in financing the unemployed youth, under-privileged sections of the society and agriculture. This was only to hammer our customer service as many high ticket customers in those days were shifting to the techno savvy private sector banks. After patiently listening to me Lt Gen remarked that State Bank is "The Bank". At the end of the meeting he got up, shook hands and sent me off with a warm smile. This incredible reception by a topmost ranking officer of the Indian Armed Forces speaks volumes of the valor and chivalry of our Armed forces. Since then I have never received a customer while seated.

Do something unique—while going through the list of my branch customers, I noticed that there were nearly 100 customers hailing from Bengal. I immediately got in touch with our Bengal Circle and requested them to send 100 calendars printed in Bangla. To the delight of the customers these Bangla calendars were gifted on the New Year. One of our very valuable customers of the rank of General Manager of a corporate client told me that this was the first time in 26 years of his banking with our branch at Hyderabad that he received a calendar in Bangla. Thank Mr. Barun Choudary our officer at Kolkata in arranging the calendars.

Customer service training-- The term *training* refers to acquisition of knowledge, skills, and competencies as a result of the teaching of vocational or practical skills and knowledge that relate to specific useful competencies (Wikipedia). It is really surprising and puzzling how only a fraction of the budget is spent on customer service training in banks. The banks spend more time on training the new employees on handling the computer rather than customer service. As a matter of fact, the employee will be required to perform more customer service at the branch. The first priority of the bank usually is to induct the employee in the organisation and fill the vacant counter and augment the staff strength. It is generally assumed that the employee will pick up customer service during the course of his work. The aim of the management is to employ a person to carry on the day to day work and assist the manager in performing her duties. The banks are well aware that repeat business is directly influenced by the service they offer to the customer. But banks even in present environment of intense market competition are more inclined to teach their new recruits systems and procedures than customer service.

Rapport helps; Rapport is feeling of trust, likeness, harmonious relation which influences our decisions. Incidentally building rapport with the customer is very important for a continuous relationship. The most widely used method is to find the likeness of the prospect.

Employee's suggestions-- Walt Disney top executives go out of their way to solicit advice from the frontline people who hear guest comments and see their reactions. Lower levels employees feel empowered when they are encouraged to voice their opinions and make suggestions.

'Kaizen'- The word 'kaizen' means "continuous improvement". It comes from Japanese word "Kai" means school and "Zen" means wisdom. Kaizen involves accepting and implementing the suggestions of the employees from the top to the lowest rung. Everyone in the company is encouraged to come up with an idea on regular basis. Each employee is expected to give 60-70 ideas in a year. These ideas are written down, shared and implemented.

Wal-Mart never hesitated to have ideas from employees at any level from loading dock workers to executives.

Manager should always take the suggestion of the employees in running the branch. Because of the employee involvement, the job of the manager becomes easier, as the employees will take upon themselves the responsibility of implementation. The functioning of the branch could be enhanced through the imagination of the employees. The employee involvement is the keystone in business development and efficient customer service.

Advantages in implementing employees' ideas,

1. They will be more open in tackling the problem.
2. They take a personal pride if their ideas are implemented.
3. It gives them job satisfaction.
4. They will be more open to discuss and accept ideas and solutions.
5. They will feel respected and increase their commitment to work.

6. The most important benefit is the involvement of the employees in running the branch.
7. This will improve attendance and quality of work.
8. If the employees feel they are contributing, they will take more active role in satisfying the customer.

Customer Suggestions---To improve the service and products customers' suggestions are necessary. It means just getting into the customer's head to know the thinking of the customer. It is mandatory for the public sector banks to place a complaints and suggestions box in the main banking hall. These locked boxes a small glass on the front a slit opening at the top for dropping the suggestions etc. this box is looked with disdain by the manager. The banks take a suggestion as a complaint. Invariably all the sites of the banks on the internet refer to suggestion and complaint and not suggestion only. The banks till 90's were without any market orientation and only accuracy was the motto to maintain customer's accounts.

When one of our customers approached our branch manager with a suggestion he was annoyed. He told the customer that he knew how to run the branch and he needed no suggestions. The customer left the bank with crest fallen face and eventually switched to another bank.

Listening and responding to customer suggestion is very vital to the functioning of a bank branch. Sam Walton, CEO of Wal-mart, walks to the customers and initiates informal conversation with them of their choice of particular item and seeks their suggestions to improve the working of the stores. The proactive manager will invite suggestions from customers on a regular basis to improve the services.

How wonderful it would be if the branch manager walks up to customers and seeks their suggestions, for improvement of the service lay out of the branch etc? Once a good suggestion comes a manager should implement it quickly. Otherwise the customer would feel disappointed and frustrated. If it is not implemented the customers should be given a convincing reason.

The banks are inward looking and are not traditionally tuned to encourage suggestions like other enterprises. The other enterprises sincerely and whole-heartedly invite suggestions from its customers to serve them better.

"WAL-MART invites suggestions. Leave your suggestions here. We are trying to let WAL-MART know that there are great ideas waiting for them in their Suggestion Box. We could use your help! Know anyone at WAL-MART? Please call or email them!"

Some of the Fortune 5 companies like Dell and Starbuck's have launched crowd sourcing sites to invite consumers to submit suggestions to improve products and customer service. This will help immensely help the company to receive millions of ideas to improve products and services at a very cheap cost.

FEEDBACK- Is to assess performance. It is a desire by a marketer or a service provider to know about the quality and performance of his service or product to serve better. Some companies are very passionate about feedback and they reward the customers for appropriate feedback. Feedback can be obtained from staff and customers. It is a communication channel between customers and the bank. It is a process of obtaining opinions from customers to be used for their benefit.

It can be described as a scanning process to know the efficiency level. It can improve our performance and highlight things that can be fine-tuned. The process of feedback involves designing of questionnaire, analysing it, chalking out action plan and implementing it. Feedback can be obtained by the front line staff from the customers orally. But the more appropriate way to obtain feedback is on printed forms so that it can be sliced, diced and implemented. Feedback form should be simple so that the customer can understand and reciprocate it without difficulty. It should not be lengthy and confusing. Only a few pertinent things should be asked in the form. Some banks in a haste to obtain feedback try to obtain a detailed opinion about its service, products, staff behavior, ambience, time taken for sanction of loan, time taken for cash receipts/payments, amenities so on and so forth. The customer may only be a depositor so he will not have any knowledge about loans. So also, there should be some incentives for a good feedback so that customer gets involved in providing honest, clear and useful feedback. Design simple feed back forms to facilitate the customer to provide instant feedback.

CUSTOMER LOYALTY

For the bank, Customer loyalty means an ability to retain customers. To build customer loyalty Banks should design programmes. Each contact with the customer is an opportunity to build customer loyalty and if this contact is not handled properly then there is a chance to lose the customer to the competitor. To attract the customer and maintain his loyalty is the biggest challenge in today's marketing environment. On a daily basis the customer is bombarded with advertisements via T.V, radio, bill boards, internet, telephone, SMS and word of mouth with tempting offers for which the customers are an easy prey and they shift loyalty.

Feedback is one of the methods to listen and respond to the customer needs. It is one of the easiest ways to listen, analyze and improve customer satisfaction through implementing good ideas.

Most of the organizations and banks are providing feedback forms on their internet sites. Accordingly, the customer will fill the columns and mention his name, account no, phone no and retransmit to the bank concerned.

Customer loyalty: Customer service and implementation of customer feedback ensure strong loyalty. Those customers who are heard and their suggestions implemented become the bank's loyal customers and evangelists to bring in more customers through word of mouth marketing. Customer loyalty can be defined as tendency of a customer to choose a product over another for a particular need. For my family consumption we buy standardized milk with 4% fat and 8% SNF (SNF contains Vitamins, minerals, protein, lactose and this is the most important part of milk) for making tea and coffee. My need for maintaining a balanced diet is to consume milk with 0% fat milk. The company which sells me milk does not sell 0% fat as such I had shifted my loyalty to the other company which sells 0% fat milk. As my need is 0% fat milk there is a shift in my loyalty. But banks nowadays are super markets with all the products available at one place. So there is very little chance of customer shifting his loyalty.

We are all in pursuit of new customers ignoring the fact that **80% of our business comes from 20% of our existing**

customers. The cost to attract new customers is significantly higher compared to maintaining relationship with the existing ones. Our efforts in building customer loyalty will certainly pay off. The banks are facing a challenge to retain customer due to credit crunch as different banks are offering different and slightly higher interest rates to attract the customers.

A loyal customer will generate more customers through referrals and promote products. A long time customer is a good candidate for cross sell and up sell because his status will increase with time. When I was a branch manager, some 20 years back, a student living in close proximity of our branch had an account with us. At present he is working as a professor in an accredited university and continued maintaining his account with us. His status has changed and he is an ideal prospect for up sale of our products. Strong personal relationships create "customer for life". Loyal customers will sing our praises to everyone they meet. Statistics shows that Banks spend 80% of their allotted resources as to attract new customers and only 20% or less on existing customers.

TIPS TO IMPROVE CUSTOMER LOYALITY

1. By training staff regularly on how to interact with the customer.
2. By making the staff learn that customer comes first for them.
3. By reaching out to them by providing information on emails, postcard, SMS, and personal contacts of your products and services.
4. Create product awareness to the staff and customers on a regular basis.

5. Attend to customer problems and complaints immediately without procrastination.

6. If you promise to deliver any product, do it on time. Be reliable. If you can't deliver it then give explanation why it was not done. You should never lose the trust of the customer.

7. Customers will always come back if the employees and manager recognize them instantly and connect with them on one to one basis.

8. Always smile when speaking with the customer whether in person or on phone.

A loyal customer will generate more customers through referrals and promote products.

3

HUG YOUR EMPLOYEES

Who comes first, it's employees or customers? Sarah cook says "**if you want to keep the customers happy you have to keep the employees happy, you can't keep the customers happy by keeping unhappy employees**." We spend more time with our employees than our family, close acquaintances and relatives. If the employees are treated like a family, you foster intimacy and informality that builds strong relationship and makes work more fun. We naturally tend to support, defend, accept and love employees more easily when they are like a part of the family. The way you treat employees the same way they will treat your customers. When the employees feel they are loved and respected they develop a great capacity to love and respect customers. The happy employee with a smile adorning his face will go a long way in making your branch's commitment to make customers happy.

Compliment employees

Some managers find it hard to compliment their employees and colleagues. They behave like policemen, always on the look out to catch employees or colleagues doing something wrong. Then they use it to their advantage. Let us not forget that we are all interdependent on our employees and colleagues for help and support. The greatest quality of true leadership is to give another person a compliment.

Simple caring words

Simple caring words make a lot of difference to the employees. For example when an employee returns after a fortnight's leave and if the manager says "we missed you" makes the employee feel important.

The assets of any leader

The assets of any leader are his followers, and the followers are not to be given commands or controlled but to be understood. To energize a branch, the manager should know the needs of the employees and respond to them. The successful manager today is the one who wins trust by sharing what she knows.

"People, products, profit…..If we take care of our people, productivity will be created, and profit will follow" (Jerry Sanders, CEO, Advanced Micro Devices). By involving the employees in the branch administration and giving them due recognition, the manager can harness and release the capabilities of the employees. The employees must know what is expected of them and receive timely, honest feedback. Excellence is expected in the quality and quantity of work done by every employee. Doing the right work, the right way saves time.

Better treatment

If a manager can treat her employees better, the branch will be ahead of their immediate competitors and dominate the market. The controllers also feel more comfortable in dealing with such amicable managers because they need results not the problems.

Jack Welch, the CEO of General Electric, once said "Any company trying to compete......must figure out a way to engage the mind of every employee."

From the employees' perspective, the manager is indeed more influential than the corporate. The manager is a catalyst in turning each employee's talent into performance. The manager who spends time with her employees is quite simply spending the most productive time. Employees inherently look for a chance to express themselves and to be recognized as individuals and to gain prestige through their expression.

Praise

It is one of the elixirs of the modern day management. The purpose of the praise is to increase productivity and employee morale. Instead of nagging the employees and creating unpleasant situations, simple praises will fetch the manager the desired results. Every employee expects appreciation every now and then and the manager should be passionate to provide it. Praise should be specific so that the employee feels that it is genuine. For instance telling the employee that because of his punctual attendance and friendly disposition there are lesser complaints. The praise should be honest and sincere as otherwise the employees can easily pickup phony praises, which will lead to the manager losing credibility and resulting in more harm than good.

Thank you

Say 'thank you' which is often overlooked. Invite employees to your home for any special event and softly praise them in front of their spouses and co-workers. When you get together with families, a pat on the back, a genuine smile will do wonders. Celebrate family day. Encourage employees to bring their families to see the workplace. Arrange picnics with the family. Present birthday cards, cakes or gifts and surprise them.

Discipline

The manager who expects **punctuality, obedience and discipline** from the employees should first set an example by adhering to these values. Setting an example is the best way in winning the respect from the employees who in turn will deliver the expected values.

To enforce discipline it is not worth threatening the employees. This may create a rift in the branch and may be you will have to eat your threats. This will be humiliating and it may affect the morale of the manager.

Listen patiently

The Manager should **listen** to the employee patiently and attentively without interfering during his deliberations. It has been observed that many times an employee just wants to get something off his chest. Listening to the employee minimizes his frustration and it communicates that you care. Listening to the employees should become a habit.

VIP treatment

Treat your employee like a VIP. Manager should visit an employee residence and familiarize with her immediate family members. Arrange discounts with the cinema theatres, places of entertainment, restaurants which interest them. Provide snacks, cold drinks, coffee on a regular basis. Whenever they engage themselves beyond working hours arrange free lunch or dinner. Manager should be sympathetic to personal problems.

Don't criticize

Sometimes we get angry when things go wrong for the mistake committed by an employee. The immediate reaction is shouting, criticizing or trying to put down the employee. We don't even wait for an explanation on how it has occurred and find remedial measures. A harsh word spoken at that time can do untold harm on the morale of that particular employee and in general on other employees.

Subordinate employee

The job of a subordinate employee (messenger) is not considered important; they too have a feeling of being in the last rung in the branch. This feeling of alienation leads to disassociation from the vision of the organization. Every job is important, whether it is cleaning toilets, sweeping the floor, arranging and stitching the vouchers etc. Imagine how a day would be if the toilets were not cleaned, the floor of the branch was not swept and the vouchers were not stitched. The messenger employees are often left to feel neglected and deprived. The manager can boost up the morale of these employees by emphasizing and appreciating their contribution for the upkeep of the branch and getting them in the team as equal partners. President Kennedy on a visit to Cape Canaveral, the space launching base of United States of America once asked an old man sweeping the floor, "What do you do here? "We are sending a man to the moon" pat came the reply, from the employee. It shows that he considered his menial job as important as any other person on the space launching base. So what ever our balance sheet speaks it is the contribution of every employee.

Managers' job

The job of managers is very complex. They are required to respond spontaneously to fast changing circumstances and deal with people at different levels. The job of the manger is to achieve the corporate objectives with the help of his employees. As a manager she will often be required to prepare the budget, present the performance of the branch to her controllers, attend regular meetings conducted at the controller's office, meeting with government agencies, attend courts and call on the customers. In such circumstances sometimes the manager will not be available to the customers, her job will be looked after by the second in command and the employees. The frontline staff are the number one players. They are the ones with direct contact with customers. The reputation and customer service of the bank rest on them. As frontline staff have direct contact with the customers, they are invaluable source of market intelligence, specific needs of customers, customer behavior and complaints. These employees need to be pampered by the manager in the friendliest way so as to have the desired results.

Manager should take a monthly feedback from the employees and try to attain the strongly agreed result on the following parameters.

1. Do I have the required knowledge of the work allotted to me?
2. Do I have the required material and equipment to work comfortably?

3. During this month did I receive any recognition or praise for my work?
4. Does my manager or supervisor take my opinion?
5. Do the manager and supervisor care for my career development?

<u>Hug employees in a nut shell</u>

- Keep the employees happy.
- Say simple caring words to the employees.
- Employees not to be controlled or commanded but to be understood
- Spend daily some time with them.
- Listen to the employees.
- Praise the employees.

4

HUGGING EXPERIENCES

Kiss your customer's dog

During one of the performance review meetings (P-review meeting), while talking about customer service, our boss suggested that the managers should be prepared even to kiss the customer's dog. None of us bothered to take it seriously. Then after a few months our General Manager came to address us and he also exhorted us to kiss the customer's dog. Then I felt it is something real which needs to be adopted. But these gentlemen did not elaborate how to kiss customer's dog. So in my anxiety to know more about it, I proceeded to British library with my membership card to refer books on the subject. I could not find any book on how to kiss customer's dog. So I approached the librarian and sought his help in the matter. He gently smiled and showed his ignorance about any such book on that subject. In my pursuit to educate my staff, I started writing an article on how to handle an irate customer, because of the delays faced by most of our customers, especially after introduction of core banking.

I had just completed the article and was browsing through it when suddenly someone forcefully pushed the door and entered my room. For a moment I was thrilled to see a tall, fair, slim, woman in a bright coloured chiffon floral printed saree which had a combination of black and red with golden border. She was certainly beautiful with large almond eyes and a broad smile that exhibited cute dimples on either side of an open mouth showing the whitest pearly teeth. I finally collected myself and managed to sputter out something that sounded like "hello". She was Mrs Susan, one of our valuable customers standing in front of me with a cute white Pomeranian puppy in her arms. Suddenly her smile turned into a frowning look and angrily asked "who is that person standing in your banking hall"? Seeing the frowning look on the customer's face I thought that this is an opportunity for me to handle an irate customer.

To handle an irate customer you should stand up with the hands on the side and lean forward so as to show that you are interested to listen. I opened the door and saw Ravi standing there and informed her that he is Mr.Ravi our branch 'grahak mitra' (Customer's friend). She sarcastically remarked "Is he grahak mitra"? She angrily said that he didn't have manners. Immediately I pulled the chair and requested her to sit. After stylishly sitting in the chair she told me that her little puppy was following her when she entered the branch and Ravi on seeing the puppy in the branch shouted 'kutte ka bacha, kutte ka bacha'(dog kid). On hearing his shouting she immediately picked up the puppy and rushed into my room to complain. She angrily explained to me that her puppy was not "kutte ka bacha", it was "kutte ka beta". She proudly told me that its name was 'ladla'. Seeing the puppy in her beautiful arms and nicely perched on her lap, I fantasized for a moment to be a puppy instead of Branch Manager a punching bag of management, employees and customers.

Then I summoned Ravi and explained to him that she was Mrs. Susan, one of our most valuable customers and the name of the puppy was 'ladla'. She interrupted me and explained to Ravi that it was 'kutte ka beta' and not 'kutte ka bacha'. She further asked him suppose Mr.Hussain (your manager) entered branch followed by his son will you say Hussain ka bacha. Ravi replied "no ma am", I will say, Mr. Hussain ka beta". Then I asked Ravi to apologize to her. If you are nice to employees they will be nice to you and will certainly carry out your instructions without hesitation. Ravi promptly said 'sorry maam'; and added in a professional P.R way, it was really a sweet kutte ka beta. She was flattered and immediately took out a cheque book of another bank and wrote a cheque for rupees thirty lakhs and asked Ravi to make a fixed deposit for three years. She candidly said "I like State Bank of India employees because if they commit mistake, they realize and readily accept it'. She told us of a similar incident in another bank, a diametrically opposite experience and therefore she now felt like transferring funds in token of appreciation of our sincere and timely apology. She annoyingly told us that the manager of that bank not only refused to offer apologies but also defended his employee by saying what was wrong as it was only a kutte ka bacha. I have decided not to bank with people who disrespect my 'ladla', she said.

Suddenly she noticed that 'ladla' was licking my table, and then she lovingly told 'ladla' not to lick the dirty table as the tables in the bank were not cleaned daily. To save my embarrassment I told her that cleaning has been outsourced in bank and every thing was cleaned daily and to impress upon her I added that my table was cleaned just an hour back. Then she lovingly asked 'ladla' to continue licking. Seeing the cheque in her hand of Rupees thirty lakhs, I told her that my side of the table was also clean and if her 'ladla' so desired it could lick my chair also.

As part of customer service and to delight children accompanying their parents to the bank I offer chocolates. I took out chocolates and offered it to the kutte ka beta. On seeing chocolates she sarcastically said "Mr. Hussain, my ladle won't eat these cheap chocolates". It likes only Cadbury Bourneville (dark chocolate. I told her that on her next visit 'ladla' will be offered Cadbury Bourneville. While I was withdrawing my hand she asked me to give those chocolates to her and I promptly obliged her. Keeping those cheap chocolates in the purse she gently said "I will give these chocolates to my husband" and went out.

And I learnt the meaning of kissing customer's dog

Didi nahi aye
(sister did
not
accompany)

I was posted as manager personal banking division in one of our branches located in a posh residential area and there is a pretty incident to narrate. As usual in the residential areas most of our customers are ladies. I used to sit in an elegantly lit cabin with big glass panes so as to have a full view of the banking hall. Whenever I saw a lady approaching my cabin I used to get up, open the door, pull the chair and ask her to sit. Then as per need write debit or credit vouchers for her. Particularly for withdrawals, I used to go to the counter take the cash, get the pass book updated and deliver the same promptly. The ladies were highly impressed. In the area some people started talking that the new manager was going steady with the ladies "ladies ko bahut line marra" (gong steady with ladies). Some of the ladies had told me that my predecessor was a 'kadooss' (very shrewd person) and he never used to allow them in his cabin. If by chance they happen to enter his cabin he immediately directed them to the counter without offering them any courtesies. These ladies were very happy with the sudden change in the attitude and functioning of the branch. One pretty lady used to often tell her husband how courteous, dashing and sweet the new manager was. After hearing about the new manager several times from his wife, he grew suspicious and sternly told her not to visit the branch any further. Then on a particular day I saw an angry young man with a very serious face entering my cabin. I immediately got up, smiled, greeted and requested him to sit. I quickly collected the pass book from him and on seeing the photo of the pretty woman, I got alarmed and immediately asked him to his surprise "Didi nahi aye" (has sister not accompanied you). He smiled and said Didi was busy with house hold chores so she could not accompany him. I asked the reason for his visit. He said that he wanted to draw Rs.10, 000/- I immediately took his cheque book, filled it and asked him to sign. Before proceeding to get cash from the counter I arranged a cup of tea. By the time he finished tea; I handed over his cash and updated pass book. His face brightened up and smilingly told me that his wife was correct about my customer service shook hands and left.

From next day onwards 'Didi'
started coming again to the bank as usual.

Eye Contact

I once impressed upon the staff to have eye contact with the customers so as to assure them that we were interested in listening to them. Eye contact is an important part of body language. If you fail to maintain eye contact during conversation it may send a wrong signal to the customer. My staff readily agreed and the very next day 'eye contact campaign' was rolled out. Since my branch was located in a residential area, a majority of the customers were ladies. As coached, my staff to the embarrassment of the ladies was directly looking into their eyes. The ladies were seen adjusting their Duppattas (stole) to avoid penetrating eye contact. One of my staff members was more enterprising in carrying out the instructions so he asked one of the lady customers. "Madam, tell me how is our customer service". She happily told "it is excellent". He further insisted, "Madam please look into my eyes and tell me how our customer service is". (Meri ankhaon may ankhein dal kar bolia humare service kaise hai). On hearing this, the lady felt embarrassed and quickly moved away. In the evening my accountant told me what had happened during the day as some lady customers had complained about unusual eye contact by the staff. I was taken aback and explained to the staff that eye contact means looking at the person but not directly into their eyes. Too much eye contact can be seen as dominating or intimidating. It should not be penetrating into the eyes of the other person. My staff was fully briefed and from then on they had eye contact without embarrassing the customers.

5

CREATING A HUGGING CULTURE

Smile

Your smile will be the first impression to customers. Smiles are an important part of communication. It is a friendly gesture and brings customer closer. A smile is just like a cherry on the topping. The customers assumes smiling employee to be friendly, caring, approachable. A smile conveys you like meeting people. A smile makes all the difference in customer service and sets the stage for transaction. Without smile you lose the first impression of hospitality. A smile is really simple, it costs nothing but it provides accessibility and congeniality. According to Martin Charnin "you are never fully dressed without a smile". If someone smiles at you, it almost makes you feel better. A smile and a warm greeting can help you to make an instant rapport.

Starbucks is the largest coffee house company in the world, with 16,120 stores in 49 countries, including around 11,000 in U.S.A. It trains staff to smile, greet and smile as part of customer service training. First impressions really count. It is a fact that customers remember what they see much more than what they hear.

Remember we are a business company and certainly cannot afford to have a neutral expression. Unfortunately neutral expressions are not neutral, they signify that you are bored, unhappy with your job and you consider customer as an interruption. Customer also loses interest in you and becomes transaction oriented. Without smile you have failed to ignite the glow in the customer for a pleasant and a memorable experience.

Start smiling and win the world.

You know me

Existing customers like to be recognized. On entering the branch the customer looks around for someone to recognize and greet him. If some employee recognizes he will approach him to get the work done. The recognition process is very effective in building relationship. If they are not recognized, they are disappointed and their relationship will be just need-based. When that's the case, the customers are vulnerable, fence-sitters and may shift their loyalty. A small mistake will also annoy them and they will not hesitate to register a complaint. They may even shout at the frontline staff to express their anger. Just get into the shoes of the customer and think about it. Who doesn't want to walk into a shop where everybody knows you by your name? When people recognize us we feel valued. We all like to be recognized. Our loyalty increases and we recommend to others. We will take our friends to do business with such organizations which understand the chemistry of human relationships.

Stay connected with customer

Powerful techniques include calling on the customer personally, face to face, by letters, calling over telephone, SMS or Email. It is important to check the customer details periodically.

Many young customers switch jobs, their residences and phone numbers. Keep updating their contact details. Put a notice in the banking hall requesting customers to provide the latest address and phone number. Make sure that you have the correct details of the customer. The customers will be too happy to provide the updated details and they will feel valued. If the phone number, email address and house address of the customer are not updated, you may not able to contact them. Subsequently you may get disconnected with the customer. BSNL informs us on phone about the due date of telephone bill and the possible disconnection for nonpayment after a certain date. The Tata sky, Vodafone, Idea mobile, Airtel all send us regular SMS about the due date and also make it a point to acknowledge the payments. Credit card companies regularly send us messages about new products and due dates of card payments. Motilal Oswal regularly sends Email to the Demat customers about latest market trends and thereby keeps connected with them. The message from all these is; always engage the customer through communication.

The more you communicate the more you get closer to the customer which creates valuable relationship.

Improving customer skills

Banks are introducing multiple technology products at a ferocious speed which provide immense convenience to the customer. The aim of the bank is to remain competitive in the market. When new technology products unfamiliar to the customers are introduced they expect us to help them use those. More significantly most of the companies teach their customers how to use their products. For example when we bought an IFB automatic washing machine, the company sent their technician to teach us to operate it. Similarly the microwave or plasma T.V. manufacturers depute their technical staff to explain us the nuances of the product for proper handling.

But consider this: when the ATM debit card was introduced most of our middle aged customers and their spouses were not able to use it for want of knowhow. My colleagues and myself in the branch used to explain our customers how to use it. Incidentally ATM was located within the premises of our branch. Some of us used to accompany them and show the operations with our cards. Later on they could operate it on their own. Customer simply loves to learn something new.

Similarly, most of our aged customers were not able to use Internet banking. My branch staff used to call on them, teach them step by step the operations. Internet banking helps the customers to pay the bills, book rail air tickets, know their balance, instruct the branch to issue cheque books, transfer funds, manage their funds and many more such things. It is anywhere, anytime banking. Once the customers learn to use the facility, they also teach their spouse, friends and colleagues. They feel immensely delighted.

Customer's education should go in tandem with the introduction of high end technology products. When phone banking was introduced a special seminar was conducted for the staff to learn the operations, so that they can teach the customers. Once the customers are taught they invariably use the product. Now the customers are operating their accounts through their cell phones. The customer needs some guidance and the branch staff should be ready to provide it.

The pay-offs from such initiatives are;

1. On learning new skills the customer is delighted.
2. It improves customer retention.
3. Traditional work of branch staff will be reduced through internet, phone banking and ATM, and they can be deputed for mobilizing more business.
4. It will become difficult for the customer to shift loyalty as it will be convenient to operate multiple products from anywhere.
5. Added to this the use of technology product is cost effective both for the bank and the customer.

Focus on most valuable customers

Customer data base is the key to the whole process of identifying valuable customers. We should be able to differentiate viable and non viable customers. Eventually every customer is important to us but some customers are more valuable than others. Those valuable customers who provide us higher share of profit should be recognized and rewarded. Success lies in identifying these customers, building relationship and seeking their help in bringing more such customers of the same profile. Understanding and knowing more about customers help us to sell easily. Our employees and colleagues can provide the lead in building and updating the data base. Recall Pareto's law, eighty percent of the profit comes from twenty percent of the customers. Once you have identified the most profitable customers, effort should be made to retain them. Maintaining excellent personalized service is the key to retain the most valuable customers. When we care for customers they hardly let us down. Learn more about their likes and dislikes. Categorize them based on age, gender, income, social status and political affiliations. It is important to get feedback from them on our products and services. Always try to act on their feed back. Be in regular touch with them. Convey the action you have initiated or taken on their feedback. They will be happy to know they are valued and reward you with their business. The need is to focus and build strong relationship. This can be built only when you know about their specific requirements and pay attention in delivering the products and services timely. The data will help us to sell, up sell and cross sell products easily, quickly and in an affordable way. Public sector Banks like any other company are focusing in increasing profit and focus should be on extending personalized service to the valuable customers rather than on commercial advertisements.

Benefits from valuable customers,

- Buy high end products.
- Pay on time without being chased for payment.
- Provide us higher share of profit.
- They will bring customers of the same profile.
- Selling to these customers is quick, easy and affordable.

Appreciation

Please don't be a miser in appreciating others. Always appreciate colleagues, employees and customers. People look for appreciation. A small word of appreciation would do wonders. Everybody remembers words of appreciation, they will tell their family members, friends and colleagues the nice words you have spoken about them. When people hear positive things about themselves they feel proud, confident and valued. Every one has an inherent desire to be appreciated for their looks, dress, car, pets, children and their passions.

Appreciating customer is an underutilized tool and a key ingredient in customer service. Appreciation will make the customers happy and grateful. You can certainly bring a smile and a glow on the customer face. Just recall in the past thirty days how many times you have appreciated a customer, employee, and colleague or you have received an appreciation. You lose nothing by appreciating others; on the contrary a foe will turn into a friend, a critic into an admirer and a hostile customer into an obliging customer.

One fact of life is that every one likes to be appreciated. When appreciation is genuine and sincere, it can move mountains. Appreciate should not be fake which makes other person consider it as flattery. Being very specific in your comments help the other person to know that you have really noticed something special and want to share. Just a simple comment like "that's a nice shirt or tie" would be enough to create from a simple conversation to an enjoyable experience for the customer. Appreciation is a powerful tool in building customer retention and loyalty.

Carolyn B. Ellis says appreciation is like a much needed rainfall to a farmer's crop that have been withering in a drought just as the crops start to shrivel and die without water, human relationships also start to feel brittle without a steady application of the nourishing, even life- giving, impacts of appreciation.

Personal attention by the manager can go a long way in making customers feel appreciated. Invariable customers will feel honored when the manager takes time to talk to them. Show the customers you enjoy meeting them and make them feel they are special. If you are friendly and charming to the customers, your staff follows suit. In your absence the same red carpet treatment will be given to the customers by your staff.

To stand out in the crowd make your branch culture more personal and unique. Some special words should be spoken by your staff to the customers like "thank you for your visit, hope to see you again". No doubt 'thank you' statements have become mechanical. Even ATM's flash out 'Thank you' after every transaction. We have become used to such statements. But never underestimate the power of personal

'Thank You'. When "thank you" is said sincerely customer will feel that you are conveying your gratitude for his business and he feel valued.

Customer today demand extra ordinary service. The difference between you and your competitor is simply courtesy and service. Train your employees to be genuine in their appreciation of your customer.

Of course, that starts at the top with you.

Pace of change

Change is part of our daily life. The pace of change has to be fast and on time. Change is a continuous process and is inevitable. We change our wardrobe and buy new clothes to align ourselves with the present fashion. We buy a new fuel efficient car to satisfy our need. Do any of us buy those rickety Fiat or Ambassador cars now? For example I bought a "VCR' a decade and half back. I did not exchange it with the 'DVD' in the market. Now my 'VCR' is outdated and obsolete. The video cassettes are not available in the market; it is just a piece of junk with me. The world's leading American auto maker General Motors, a 100 year old company filed bankruptcy as a result of competition from efficient Japanese firm like Toyota. Even patriotism is not helping the auto giant to persuade its customers to buy American own company product. When the need arises the customer thinks beyond patriotism. We see daily that many companies and products just disappear from the market. The reason: they did not keep pace with change. It is obvious that change will increase flexibility and effectiveness to keep us ahead in the competition. As Orlan Boston, senior manager with Deloitte has said "Companies don't transform themselves just for fun, but to stay competitive, innovative, and operationally effective".

People don't easily accept change. Just recollect when the cell phone was introduced in the market. A lot of people thought it to be crazy. Interestingly many physicians talked about its radiation effect on the users. Managers thought if they are provided with cell phones they will be disturbed even at home. In the beginning it was really expensive. Slowly it got the attention of the customers and now most of us possess the cell phone and we feel uncomfortable without it. The same thing happened with our 'ATM' card. Our elderly customers were not willing to use it. They preferred face to face transaction. It took some time for us to convince these customers the benefit of using 'ATM' cards. Now we know that the industry thrives on change and the pace of change is more important for a better and profitable future.

Pressure on the PSU banks to change has come from private sector and foreign banks. Just see how the banking has remarkably changed during the last decade. But it is really great that the PSU banks accepted the challenge of change more particularly the largest bank of the country State Bank of India. With initial hiccups they geared up to train its employees and implement the latest technology. The present story of the Bank is quite different and encouraging. It has not only arrested but tremendously improved its market share to remain at the number one position.

This is certainly due to upgrading and implementing new technologies to keep pace with the change.

Giving the glow

The customer is not just looking for your product or service; it is available to him in any other bank. They go to the place where people are cheerful, radiate positive energy and are enthusiastic in carrying out their work. Nobody would like to deal with a person with a frozen dull face without a smile and is least cheerful. A glowing person radiates not only positive energy but he spreads it to other person. Like the famous proverb "one candle enlightens the other" so also the glowing person spreads joy and enthusiasm among his colleagues. Research has shown that happy employees are more productive than unhappy employees. They enjoy work and keep customers and colleagues happy. They bubble with enthusiasm, inspire, excite and ignite others. They just glow. They are pleasant, cheerful, happy and positive lot. They attract customers like honey attracts the bees. By being cheerful they create value addition to customer service. Customer recognizes the bank through its people. If the people in the bank are cheerful, customers feel comfortable and at home. Identify the customer's requirements and deal with them in an efficient and courteous manner. If they give the customer better enjoyable experience he will feel inseparable and a part of the family. It is important to remember that you are in a direct position to win or lose business for your bank. It is equally important for the manager to create an environment where every employee is happy and cheerful. We should pack up our personal worries during business hours and refrain from telling others.

The employees have to go an extra mile to capture the heart of the customer.

Lagniappe

Lagniappe is pronounced as "lan-yap". The meaning is a little bonus that a friendly shopkeeper may add to the purchase or something extra offered as a means to please the customer. Getting more than expected, a little more than paid for is "lagniappe". Most of us might have experienced that the groundnut (peanuts) seller throws something extra after a measure. So also the vegetables seller throws some extra green chilies or green coriander after every purchase. My wife and I sometimes go to buy vegetables and she skips some shops. Once I asked the reason for skipping those shops. She told me that those shopkeepers are very miser and they don't give any extra. Certainly we resist going to a shop where that extra scoop is not added to our purchase. Lagniappe is something extra in customer care and customer service to every customer. It is part of the customer service to woo and attract customers for repeat purchase. I had once accompanied my son to Pizza-hut and ordered pizzas. For nearly 5 minutes the order was not served but before we could remind the server he placed a plate of ginger bread due to delay in serving the pizza. This was something unexpected for which we were not charged. So also some of the banks give one credit point to every purchase of Rs.100 through its "ATM" cards. Likewise many banks, credit card companies offer bonus points and free accident insurance to satisfy the customers.

Customer in today's competitive environment expects more than ever before. "Lagniappe" need not always be extra peanuts, green chilies or ginger bread but also it can be a sincere effort to help the customer. For example a customer comes and intends to have a term deposit; find out why he intends a term deposit. Try to get the details as far as possible so that you can suggest some better alternative to meet his needs. He can get better returns from mutual funds, SBI life products and other products of the bank or its partners than term deposit. If the employee is able to explain other products from which the customer can get more benefit, the customer may accept his suggestion. This unexpected something viz extra effort which the customer had not expected is "lagniappe". Interestingly customer service is full of opportunities. It is the opportunity of outsmarting the competitor with a service that provides something unexpected and extra. Friendly, innovative, emphatic staff will provide a pleasant experience to the customer.

**Always focus on something extra
to delight the customer.**

Under promise and over deliver

It means when someone promises to deliver by evening and then delivers in the afternoon thereby exceeding the expectations of the customer. The idea behind this concept is to keep the expectations of the customers low and then exceed it. Managing customer expectations goes a long way in achieving customer satisfaction and delight. On the other hand, if some one is promised certain service which is not delivered on time, he will invariably get irritated and infuriated.

For example, to get a replacement of my damaged remote set, I contacted on telephone Tata sky satellite television. The executive promised to change the remote within 24 hours. After I hung up my land line telephone there was a SMS message on my cell phone indicating my complaint number and also service engineer mobile number. In my anxiety immediately, I contacted the service engineer and he informed that he was on his way to my residence to attend the request. Within an hour he reported at my residence, checked my remote and replaced it as it was beyond repair. I was delighted for such a quick service even though the company had promised twenty four hours. This is an example of under promise and over delivery.

These are the advantages of under promise and over delivery,

When the product is delivered on time as promised, it pleases the customer. Customer will speak to others positively about you and your promptness. The bank will be able to retain customers.

This will make the customers happy and delighted.

Remember: always under promise and over deliver to delight the customers.

My colleagues who helped me to create a hugging culture are too numerous to mention here but some of them whose names are stuck to my mind are, S.A.Karim, P.V.Sreedhar, K.J.Srinivas, H.Shankar, R.Adam and P.Ravi.

6

CELEBRATION AND RECOGNITION HELP

Celebrations help friends and colleagues to get together and spend the time merrily. When we achieve some mile stone, there is something inside us that screams out and says "let's celebrate". Celebrations are what we do at home. Children's birthday, marriage anniversary, celebrating son's or daughter's success in the examination, a new born baby, our promotion, etc. We all celebrate any significant event in the lives of our family members. Similarly at the branch also it should be a regular affair, the way we do in the family. Celebrations should be with full zest, enthusiasm and vitality. Celebrations help to attract and retain employees, and most important, keep them motivated and dedicated. Celebration need not be expensive; it can be as simple as a sincere appreciation or presenting a card. But it works.

Celebrate the birthday of employees

Present a birthday card, order a cake and make her cut it in the morning in the presence of all the employees. Make sure that everybody in the branch greets her. Present a suitable gift to the birthday baby. This would enliven the atmosphere in the branch and every employee will look forward to his/ her turn and the celebrations that would follow.

Celebrate every month

Every month celebrate the service rendered by the employees who go above and beyond the ordinary and make a true difference in customer care. Don't just highlight the employee's work but design a recognition program with the help of other employees. Managers build loyalty when they celebrate the employee's success.

Compliments act as nutrients just like fertilizers for plants. If you have not tried this, please try now in your branch,

1. Punctual employee of the month. (On various fronts)
2. Highest number of payments/receipts in a month.
3. Highest number of pass book printing in a month.
4. Prompt day book checking.
5. Best dressed person of the month.
6. Highest number of accounts opened in a month.
7. Customers call at home.
8. Man/ woman of the month.
9. And many more can be added.

Employee's children

Celebrate the achievements of the employees' children. Feel and share the happiness of others wholeheartedly. Invite them to the branch and felicitate them for their excellent performance in examination, sports, games, painting, obtaining job and in many more such achievements. Present them letter of appreciation, and a memento. This will help the manager build relationship with the employees' families.

Send a write up

Celebrate the achievement by sending a write up of performance of the employee to house magazines along with her photo. Put on the notice board the story of performance carried in the house magazine so that customers can also see how the employees are performing. The performance should be highlighted when senior executives visit the branch. This will help achieve continuous improvement in levels of quality and customer service.

Money is not the criteria

It is generally believed that the only thing the employees want is money. Many studies have shown that money is not the criteria for rewards. More of importance to employees are the intangibles such as being appreciated for the work done, keeping them informed about the opportunities available for career development, listening about their suggestions and implementing them, providing a feeling that they are not ignored. They need to be reassured that they are the important employees of the bank. When big money is involved as a prize, lot of things will creep in leading a win lose attitude by hiding of the facts, mistrust, misleading, refusing to help others, screw the other guy, etc the only intention of the employee will be winning. But for a small prize like a T-shirt employees will put in untiring efforts to win if the contest is meaningful and the manager is sincere.

Prizes are treasure

What happens when the employees receive a prize? These prizes will be placed in the showcase in their drawing rooms.

In showcases there will be trophies, mementoes, small cups, won by them or their children. They will never tire of showing these to the guests. So every prize given to the employee is worth because he will treasure it, remember his performance and show it to others. What gets rewarded gets repeated.

EMPLOYEES APPRECIATION DAY

In USA first Friday of March is celebrated as employee's appreciation day. When we are celebrating valentine day, Halloween day, mother's day, father's day, friendship day, why can't there be an employees appreciation day? My hearty congratulations to those managers who celebrate employee appreciation day. If you are a manager then you will know how important it is to motivate employees and keep them in good humor. An employee deserves all the thanks in the world. It is not a fun day but it should be a recognition and appreciation for employee satisfaction. Employees who are appreciated are more positive towards work and they feel confident. A manager should create an environment of recognition, rewards and celebration. In communication, nonverbal communication is 93 % and verbal is only 7%. Use proper body language to communicate with the employees. That means your body language is richer in expression than the words. Here are a few examples of body language that will send positive nonverbal messages:

1. Smile.
2. Make eye contact.
3. Stand straight.
4. Don't move while speaking.

Praise should be sincere, specific, meaningful and immediate

Women employees deserve all our appreciation and gratitude for creating work- home balance. They are sincere, honest, hardworking and very congenial. They have a dual responsibility of managing the home, caring for the children and attending to their home work, assignments, reading stories to them and earning a living. Woman shapes the character of our future citizens. If she has to sit late in office, note to gift her family pack (food) so that she need not cook after reaching home. Celebrate women's day in a big way. Invite women customers, elaborate the new schemes for them and take suggestion for improving the service.

PEET PROGRAMME: At Paul Revere insurance group conducts the "THE PEET" program. It stands for "program for ensuring that everybody's thanked". This program was developed to improve commitment and enthusiasm of the employees. Each of the top 15 executives of the company was given the names of two quality leaders to personally visit each week, and talk anything. Interesting things happened, the executives enjoyed the unstructured meetings and they learned a great deal about the employees who made up their companies. Visiting the employees, listening to them and learning from them became the culture of the company and the corporate culture changed from down side up. Earlier all the ideas for change came from senior managers and after this program it was concluded that any one in the organization can do the right thing.

How celebration and recognition helps:

1. Celebrations help connectivity in the branch among employees and their families.
2. Celebration de-stresses the fatigue built around routine work.
3. Celebrations inspire and rejuvenate employees.
4. Celebrations create joy and aliveness amongst employees and their families.
5. Recognition creates the feeling of being special and motivates to take up the challenge.
6. When people are recognized they feel better about themselves and develop more dedication towards work.
7. Recognition makes the employees happy that their efforts are recognized.
8. Appreciation makes the employee work excitedly and this decreases absenteeism.
9. It helps the employee work harder and improves the competitiveness of the organization.
10. Create a wall of fame – paste the photographs of the employees taken on different occasions of recognitions and celebrations.

Celebrate all the festivals like Diwali, Dashera, Ramzan, Christmas, Bangla, Tamil, Telugu, Gujarati New year. Put banners for the New Year in the respective language. This will surprise the customers and improve loyalty.

7

HOUSE KEEPING

The ambience must be inviting, where a customer will feel comfortable. If the work place looks shabby, cob-webs hanging from the roof, toilets foul smelling with graffiti on the walls, furniture dusty, glasses not properly cleaned, what impression you will leave on the minds of the customer. Banks are nowadays spending quite a huge amount on the ambience by renovating the branches with vitrified tiles, ultra modern single window counters, Venetian blinds, new electric fixtures, curtains, sofas for the convenience of the staff and the customer. There are certain chores to be done every day while some others, weekly, to keep the premises clean and attractive. Plan to carry your housekeeping plan regularly and systematically to delight the customers. You should be passionate to keep your premises clean the way a housewife keeps her home clean and tidy. Generally cleaning, mopping, and vacuuming is done daily. Then arrange for washing curtains, drapes, polishing furniture and cleaning light fixtures on weekly or monthly basis. Obviously there are benefits in maintaining cleanliness. A clean and well kept premise attracts customers.

McDonald's Corporation is the largest chain of fast food restaurants catering to 47 million customers daily in 119 countries. Their operating philosophy is based on QSC&V formula-representing quality, service, cleanliness and value.

They are superb in cleanliness from kitchen, dining room to the parking lots. If you visit their restaurant in your neighborhood you will always find a worker neatly dressed mopping the floor. Cleanliness helps achieve hundred percent customer satisfaction.

As the saying goes, first impression is the best impression. Attractive surroundings for both staff and customers provide the feel good factor. Just imagine how much nice it is to sit in a banking hall with freshly painted walls, comfortable chairs, a beautiful painting, a decent flower vase, light refreshing music and latest magazines. The moment customer enters the branch he will be certainly impressed with the orderly setting of your premises. Neat, tidy premises will have a soothing effect on customers and help calm the nerves. Interestingly it will be easy to deal with customers.

Research by color psychologist Dr David Lewis showed that the staff believes the color of their surroundings has a significant impact on both their emotions and their performance. He found blue was all round winner for enhancing mood and helping brain function, while red increased mental agitation and tension. It also affects the mood of the customers. Isn't it amazing that a simple thing like the color of our office affects the mood of the customers and the staff?

"Light affects mood and alertness by shutting down the production of melatonin, the sleep inducer," says Dr.Howard. Alertness is important for safety and productivity more particularly in banks. The work environment should be well lit. As such darkness or dim lighting triggers the pineal gland to secrete melatonin, which increases the feeling of sleepiness.

Fragrance also plays an important role in the branch set up. We all like fragrance. We all know the smell of fuel and oil in car repair garages, nauseating stench public toilets as also the fragrance of religious places. It is a well known fact that fragrance has certain good effects on our emotions. The fragrance can actually set the mood, not only romantic way but also peaceful way. Our ancestors knew the importance of fragrance in their daily lives, including in spiritual and medicinal practices. Use effectively, regularly good air fresheners, and incensed sticks which neutralizes and destroys offensive odours. Fragrance is a subtle but powerful mental stimulant; it helps foster a sense of well being, energy and creativity. Fragrance will have a magical affect on soothing the emotions of the customers and will make it easier for us to interact.

Tom Peters says "become housekeeping fanatics". Carl Sewell says customers judge us on just about everything. And making sure the restroom (toilet) is immaculate and tastefully decorated is another way for us to underscore our concern for them, and another way to differentiate ourselves from the competition. Put a picture or a painting in the rest room.

Recall how we arrange naphthalene balls in wash basins, urinals and sanitization during the period of inspection of our branches. If the toilets are not clean and sanitized there is a chance that the branch inspector would comment in the inspection report and it may even affect inspection rating. These are simple things but they matter a lot to the customers and staff. The staff and customer rest rooms should be immaculate, properly sanitized with some paintings on the wall to delight staff and customers.

Inspect the staff dinning room regularly. Provide clean plates, water, adequate chairs and tables. There you and your staff dine after a day's hard work. Let them enjoy the experience. There is so much you can do.

Tips for housekeeping,

1. Is the name board (signage) clean, clear, unbroken and creating a right image of your bank.
2. Are the air fresheners and incensed sticks being used?
3. Whether the building is clean from outside.
4. Are the customer chairs comfortable for sitting?
5. Are there newspapers, magazines, T.V, music available for the customers?
6. Are the customer toilets clean, sanitized and well equipped?
7. Is the water cooler functioning?
8. Is the lighting sufficient?
9. Are the vouchers available and kept neatly in a shelf.
10. Are there sufficient writing tables for the customers?
11. Check and recheck these and such other things every day to create a memorable experience for the customer and the staff.

Waiting time

We wait in lines every day. We wait behind others in the banking hall for transactions. We wait in queues for updating our bank passbook. We wait on phone to talk to our service representatives. We wait in railway station to purchase a ticket. We wait in the shopping malls to pay our bills. Even though we are used to waiting, we hate it. Undoubtedly we all hate to wait. Waiting is frustrating because we have so many other things to do in our lives.

Customers lose patience for long waiting. The first direct interaction between bank and the customer is waiting time. Studies have shown that 80% customers walk out of restaurant. 40% left a bank, and 50% walked out of a convenience store because the wait was too long. And for those walked out- 30% of them never went back. But do you know that the customers are forgiving for the wait times if the employees are courteous, genuinely sorry for the inconvenience and all smiles? Customers become very unhappy when the first come first serve principle is violated. Customers at a bank were found to be dissatisfied when they saw employees at windows doing activities other than attending on the waiting customers. Customer feel frustrated when employees are busy speaking on the phone while they waited. Counters that are not staffed make customers feel the bank was understaffed. If the bank has six counters, customers expect to see all the six in operation during peak hours.

As Levitt says "products are consumed, services are experienced". Since unoccupied time feels longer than occupied waiting time, keep customers occupied with something interesting which can reduce the perceived waiting period. A study revealed that offering something to look at during waiting improved the customers' attitude. The aim is to take the customer's mind off the waiting. Even a simple mirror in front of them works as they could spend sometime enjoying the image of the most important person in their lives (read themselves).

Why do you want your customers to wait? Are you giving something special which they do not get in another place?

If you make your customers wait unnecessarily, they will certainly leave. Maybe not today maybe not tomorrow but they will leave. Sooner or later, but surely they will leave. They will leave at the first opportunity.

A friendly employee can take off the pressure of waiting by smiling and chatting with the customer. Try to segment high ticket and valuable customers for easy transaction. If customer experience unexpected delays, explain the reasons for the delay. Passengers who were told why their flight was delayed indicated higher satisfaction than the passengers who were not informed.

My staff often used to complain that customers get irritated waiting for a few minutes in our bank whereas they wait for hours in the cinema hall to buy ticket. To see the picture of their liking is a desire and this is called a 'big payoff' whereas to transact the business in the bank is a necessity, particularly as they draw their own money. For example in the case of customers who avail loan they don't mind waiting longer for release of the loan amount. The more valuable the service, the longer the customer will wait.

So what can you do to reduce perceived waiting time?

- Music provides a pleasant atmosphere but it fails short to influence their perception of waiting.
- Install T.V in the banking hall to take off the pressure of waiting.
- Keep newspapers and latest magazines for reading.
- Inform the customers of the waiting time.

- Try to see all the counters in the banking hall are staffed.
- Arrange a computer for internet banking.

To satisfy and relieve the waiting time banks have now installed more than one ATM in the same place.

It is necessary for the banks to seriously address waiting experience- one that is more pleasurable and less frustrating.

Office Dress code

There is an old saying "you should eat the food you like and wear dress which others like". For bankers office is a second home where we spend a sizeable amount of waking hours. Considering that your office dress should match the status of workplace ethics and is also convenient to you. The manager and the employees should wear the right dress to be presentable. The dress should be neat, clean, pressed and appropriate for the daily office use. There is a fixed dress code for certain professions but it is free for all in the banking industry. It should be borne in mind that attire of a person speaks volumes about his image and culture. The dress adds an image of professionalism and reflects a strong personality.

Men should be well shaven, with properly groomed hair. Unshaved people look sick and this will send a wrong signal to the customer and colleagues. Care should be taken not to wear casual dress like kurta (loose shirt) pajamas and t-shirts or jeans in the office. Manager should indulge in power dressing. In metros he should be in suitable branded shirt, pant, tie and shoes in perfect coordination. The shirts must be light colored, not flashy, pants dark colored with a suitable belt and a mild perfume like Hugo bass, berberry or escada sport. The tie again should not be flashy, have a double perfect tie knot that reaches the belt. The tie should not be too long or short and the tie knot should not be loose. Proper tie knot projects confidence. The dress of the manager as their leader helps in building confidence in the employees and draws respect from the customers.

Dos,

- Shave daily and keep hair neatly trimmed.
- Wear light colored shirts and dark pants.
- Manager should sport tie with a proper knot.
- Black Shoes are the best with laces.
- Socks should match the pant.
- If you wear perfume, keep it mild.
- Wear well fitted dresses.

Don'ts

- Never wear a t-shirt, kurta pajama (this is for politicians) or sports shoes in office.
- No glazy tie pins or big buckles belts.
- Don't undo the buttons of the shirt.
- Don't grow nails and hair.
- Don't use heavy perfumes disturbing others.
- Don't wear white socks.
- Avoid half sleeved shirt.

The ladies who, by and large are dress conscious, wear suitable dresses. Dress of a woman has come a long way from traditional sari to Shalwar khameez and western dress. There is no doubt that shalwar (loose trousers) khameez (ladies long shirt) scores some points over sari in comfort and convenience but the latter is more alluring than any other dress. Sari offers style, dignity and respect for the wearer. Chiffon and georgette saris are elegant with pearls. Labels like splash, Sumeet Suri, Allen solly and many other popular men brands also cater to western dresses for modern, stylish women executives. These labels offer trousers, jackets, shirts in appealing colors from black, beige to pastel. It is advisable to avoid dangling earrings, heavy jewelry, tight fitting revealing and flashy clothes.

8

HUG SENIOR CITIZEN

In Indian society senior citizens enjoy status within the society that is unparalleled elsewhere in the world. The generations born in the early 1950s have come of age. They are wealthier, better informed about health and lifestyle, and technologically more literate than their predecessors. Age invariably has a noticeable effect on the needs of a consumer. Nevertheless, even for a market that involves everyone, segmentation by age is often relevant because it facilitates more finely tuned approach for effective marketing and advertising for the aged. According to the predictions of US Census Bureau, between 1997 and 2025 the world population will increase by 36%, during which time the number of people aged 60+ will grow by 112% and those aged 80+ by more than 125%. The improvement in life expectancy is incredible. This is very vital information for banks and insurance companies to offer products and services to this segment of the population. As far as lifespan is concerned, since the beginning of the twentieth century the inhabitants of developed countries have seen, on an average 30 years added to their life expectancy. Certainly this century will see greater progress in life expectancy.

Marketing for particular segment

In this era of laser guided missiles or 'the surgical strikes' marketing for particular segments is vital instead of mass marketing for all. The banks need products which will satisfy the needs and aspirations of the senior citizens. It is reasonable to think that people after retirement will be spending more than two decades of their lives happily indulging in their pursuits of better living. All the stress built during the eat-work-sleep years gives way to a new rhythm. Most of these people after retirement are debt free, and because of their saving habits, have much more disposable income compared to the struggling, spend thrift, credit prone ambitious younger generation. This over ambitious, spendthrift younger generation has sent many economies of the world into recession.

Moneyed grand parents

As there are many moneyed grandparents they will enjoy their leisure with grandchildren. This has got the attention of McDonald's in its worldwide campaigns which invested millions of dollars in advertisement that features grandparents with their grand children in their restaurants. Disney too also runs campaigns that feature grandparents with grand children. Many American retail chains, banks, insurance Companies and hotel chains have embarked on vast training programmes for staff to handle the over 50 age customers.

Stable customers

One of the best commercial advertisements on TV is of SBI Life Insurance which features a bunch of very old retirees playing cricket and telling an irritated young boy that they have worked a lot and they have now plenty of time to play. Banks will now have to gear up to understand the needs of these stable customers. Banks should understand that the wealth these senior customers have accumulated during a lifetime of work is too precious to be put at risk. The senior citizens are very serious about information. They ask questions testing the patience of the seller, collect brochures, leaflets and they minutely scan them before taking any decision to purchase. They have immense appetite for information and lend their ear to the person who treats them respectfully. It is an appropriate time that banks trained its staff to handle senior citizens efficiently.

Banks should target these customers with specially designed products and provide better amenities in the branches.

9

MARKETING

In the recent times there has been a great awareness in the Indian banking industry for marketing the products and services. Marketing is now a buzzword in the banks and eventually all the banks are now geared towards marketing. After the economic liberalization in 1991 the private sector banks with high technology orientation, set the tone of marketing in financial products and services. The public sector banks were jolted and exposed to intense competition in technology and customer service.

Everyday and everywhere people talk about marketing. Generally in my sessions I ask the definition of marketing and most of the participants give the description of marketing confusing it with selling. So I ask them to remember a simple definition by Philips Kotler, the marketing guru, "meeting needs profitably", because remembering long definition at an advanced age is a bit difficult. Once you tell this definition you are through and if you add 'Philips Kotler' name to the definition you have further successfully sealed the answer. S.H.Simmons, humorously defines marketing in an anecdote. If a young man tells his date 'she's intelligent, looks lovely, and is a great conversationalist', he's saying the right thing to the right person and that's marketing.

Eugene Jerome McCarthy classified marketing mix in the early 1960s into four broad groups that he called the 4 P's of Marketing. They are product, price, place and promotion.

1. Product

Customers satisfy their needs and wants through product. Usually the product is a physical object, such as a car, T.V, fridge, microwave or could be a financial product like savings bank account, fixed deposit, life insurance, mutual funds, etc. Products are both tangible and intangible. The intangibles are the ones which the customers get through service which satisfies their needs and wants. We buy the product not only to possess it but also to get benefits out of it.

Big companies spend enormous amounts to know the needs of the customers. A study conducted by John Koten says that most big companies have answers to all the what, where, when and how questions about the customers' buying behaviors. Among other things they even know that our favorite toothbrush color is blue. They also know our affordability to buy the product. For example in rural markets because of low income big companies provide products of daily use like shampoo, hair oil, toothpaste and many other items in small sachet at affordable price. Basing on our needs and likes they create products. For a product to be successful there has to be proper segmentation to meet the specific requirement of the customer. Just like a Mercedes Benz car for the high income group and a nano car with comparatively low income for the common man. Products can be classified into durable, non durable and services.

- a. **Durables goods;** are those goods which are used for long periods like fridge, television, car and furniture.
- b. **Nondurable goods**; are those goods which are consumed in one or a few uses like soap, toothpaste, milk, etc.

c. **Services-** Are activities which offer benefits or
satisfaction. For example the customer comes to buy
a product like fixed deposit in a bank; he also values
the quality and speed of the service. Whether the
staff treats him with courtesy, is they enthusiastic in
their job and serves him with a smile. It is because
the customer wants and expects excellent service all
the time.

2. Pricing

There is a price for every product and service one avails. We
pay a price to buy a fridge, cell phone, book, and car and also
for availing services from banks to obtain a demand draft, pay
order, bank guarantee and a local short credit. Price is a source
of revenue and it generates profit for the company, entities
and also for individuals. Pricing is based not only on cost,
quality, and affordability of customers but also the reaction
of the competitors. Significantly the price of a product and
service has to be reasonable in comparison with that of the
competitor's price. In banks particularly pricing is done for
both assets and liability products under close monitoring of
R.B.I. The R.B.I monitors prices taking into consideration the
overall development of the economy and also to control the
inflationary trends. Unlike product, price is a flexible element
and it can be changed easily. Internet provides immense access
to the customers to compare the price of the products of various
competitors. There are various terms used for pricing, a few
of which are;

a. **Market penetration pricing-** Is an attempt by a
company to capture or increase its share in the market.
This is often offering low price than the competitor to

draw customers. Some banks adopted this strategy to increase their market share in housing and car loans.

b. **Market skimming pricing-** The latest price skimming is of iPhone in India. In a country where there are one billion cells phone subscribers and the market has reached a saturation point and the growth is slow in the first Quarter of 2015.At the beginning of 2015, CEO of Apple Tim Cook has said that the sale of IPhone is well ahead of China. The prices of these phones are as high as Rs.31,000.00 for 8 G-byte version and Rs.36000.00 for 16 G-byte versions. Price skimming is done by some companies to test the market and the products are targeted for high end customers. It also helps the company to build a niche market of status conscious customers who try to purchase the product at exorbitant price. Then the companies slowly bring down the prices after creating 'status symbol' brand. Some companies also aim at extracting maximum returns from the customers for the new technology product before competitors emerge.

c. **Promotional pricing-** Is to launch products in below the line marketing campaigns. Banks, during festive seasons, temporarily offer housing and car loans without processing charges. This has become a regular feature to attract customers. Banks also offer, for a specified period, higher interest rates to mop up their deposits.

d. **Psychological pricing -** For example some commodities like brown eggs command premium price than the white eggs. The customer has a perception that the brown eggs are more nutritious than the white eggs and pays premium price for it. Some consumers, particularly women, while buying saris perceive higher priced saris to have higher quality and they prefer to buy those.

3. Place

How the product does reach the customer? It should be available to the customer at the right time, at the right place and in right quantity. The product has to be available and accessible to the consumers, otherwise you lose the sale. It also refers to the channel by which a product or service is sold and to which segment (young, families, business people). It also includes how it is to be transported to reach the customers on time.

4. Promotion

This is done through advertising, viz., T.V, Radio commercials, publicity, sales promotion, branding and various other methods of promoting the product. It is to stimulate and attract the customer to purchase the product through various advertising channels. It is to build consumer demand for the product. Daily we are bombarded with hundreds of advertisements over T.V, radio, news papers, magazines, bill boards and even on the T-shirts of sports persons. We often come to know the features and the benefits of a product through advertisements. It is a pull strategy to induce the prospect to buy the product.

The 7Ps or extended marketing mix of Booms and Bitner is a marketing strategy tool that expands the number of controllable variables from the 4 Ps in the original marketing mix model to 7. The traditional marketing mix model of 4 Ps was primarily directed for tangible products. The 7 Ps model is useful for services industries.

The other three additional Ps added by Booms and Bitner are

1. People

All people directly or indirectly involved in the service, encounter the bank's front line employees, officers', B.C/B.Fs, other contact agents and customers. Banks depend on its frontline employees to deliver the services to the customers. The frontline employees and officers are the most important people in delivering quality service and creating a favorable image for the bank. A satisfied customer is just not looking for the right product at the right time and the right place. The customer also wants cordial reception, courtesy, accuracy and speed. The winning companies help the employees in providing customer satisfaction by adequately training them in customer service. Personalized service is a key element in customer satisfaction, long term customer relation and customer loyalty. An excellent customer service will influence customer perception and a repeat purchase.

2. Process

Is referred to the procedures, mechanisms and flow of activities by which the service is delivered. This involves a sequence of steps and activities. In a branch situation customers stand in a queue to be attended for payments, receipts or buying drafts/bankers cheques and paying challans (Government payments). If it takes more than expected time of the customer he will be annoyed. In case of a loan there are certain procedures and mechanism to be followed. The combination of these steps constitutes a service process which is evaluated by the customer. The management should take proper steps in reducing the delivery time of the service to create a customer oriented approach.

3. Physical evidence

This includes both tangible and intangibles. The tangible includes brochures, letterheads, signage, internet, lighting, ambience, seating arrangement, cleanliness as well as appearance and attitudes of the employees. The physical facilities play an important role in the service experience. The intangibles are the experience of the existing customers and the ability of the business to provide satisfaction to potential customers. Credit cards are one of the examples of tangible that provides credit (intangible) by the credit card companies and banks. In fact physical environment is part of the product itself. The customer feels and values under what environment the product was delivered. He assesses the strength of the bank through the physical assets like ambience, furniture and equipment.

Below the line marketing (BTL)

Is for specific and limited group of customers. Most of the banks organize home loan, car loan and education loan fairs for specific target groups. In these times of recession many companies and banks are going in for BTL because they are cost effective in getting across the customer than through normal media channels. Sometimes the companies hold press conferences and invite media personnel to show their products through which they get media coverage at a very inexpensive way. The advertisement on T.V is expensive and studies have shown that while watching T.V the viewers will be constantly switching the channels avoiding advertisements. Remote has given them the power and choice of what and when to watch. Recently in T20 world cup of 2009 the TRP has suddenly fallen because of the exit of the Indian team from the tournament. This has resulted in huge losses to most of the advertising companies.

Whereas in BTL method of marketing the customers are persuaded vigorously by the staff and interest discounts are also offered for a limited period on booking during these melas (fest). It is verbal and face to face interaction with the prospect to induce buying. Certainly personal selling provides push to the product. Many of our branches hold specific loan fortnights or participate in the local fair and melas to attract and sell the products.

BTL is the best approach in rural marketing because in India around 25000 melas(fest) are held every year and interestingly in some of the melas the attendance is more than a crore (10 million). Now a day's all the multinational companies are heading towards the melas and Haats (village market) to set up their stalls to give a 'touch and feel experience' of their products. The most common among them are Eicher tractors, Britannia biscuits, Hindustan Uni Lever, Escorts, FMCG's (fast moving consumer goods) and many more such companies.

Many companies are finding cheaper routes of marketing like paintings on the walls, arranging puppet shows, folk songs, and folk theatre. More enterprising companies like Nokia are trying to reach rural markets where 812 million people live with 'show room on wheels' and also tie up with micro finance to have a better reach in the rural market. Several companies are opting for video vans for publicity in the rural markets to have a direct reach with rural customer instead of advertisements on T.V, radio and news papers. But for big companies it compliments their ATL (above the line) campaigns.

Organize BTL marketing through,

1. Email,
2. Mail, (leaflets)
3. Events,
4. Telephone,
5. SMS,
6. Put stalls at rural fairs, Haats,
7. Arrange contacts at schools, colleges, Government offices, universities and hospitals,
8. Public relation campaigns,
9. Meetings.

Above the line marketing (ATL)

Promotional activities carried out through mass media such as T.V, Radio, news paper are classified as 'above the line' promotions. It is tailored for the mass audience but more and more companies are finding it expensive as the rates of advertising through the mass media are soaring very high day by day. But no company can dare avoid mass media because of its reach. No doubt advertisements influence purchasing to some extent by repeatedly reminding the customer of the company's products. More often the company also wants to demonstrate its power and control in the market through attractive big splash advertisements; and also to lift the brand.

These ATL are more suitable for the urban audience because of their busy, exhausting life style. In short ATL marketing is for big ticket items. ATL marketing tends to be difficult to measure from the returns as compared to BTL.

Examples of ATL category include,

1. Television.
2. Radio.
3. Newspapers.
4. Bill boards.
5. Magazines.

WORD OF MOUTH MARKETING: Refers to inter personal communication about commercial entities. It is an act of telling at least one friend, acquaintance or family member about a satisfactory or unsatisfactory product or service experience. Philips Kotler says word of mouth is the only promotion method that is of consumers, by consumers and for consumers.

We are daily bombarded with not less than 2000 advertisements on T.V, newspapers, magazines, bill boards, on cabs, auto rickshaws and everywhere. But to purchase particularly long value-based products like T.V, fridge, washing machine, car, micro wave, etc, we ask our relatives, friends, colleagues and an acquaintance. We build a perception of the product. When we visit the showroom to buy, already a preconceived perception is in the mind about the product and we are not carried away by the persuasion of the salesman for any other competitive product. Generally we buy the product which was referred to us by others.

They are two types; one is negative word of mouth ((NWOM) complaining to friends, colleagues and relatives about unsatisfactory experience with a product or service. In contrast, positive word of mouth marketing (PWOM) is about information of satisfaction of a product or service. Analysts have viewed that **NWOM** is more lethal and potent than **PWOM**.

With word of mouth marketing channel, there is good news and bad news, the good news is that you don't have to pay to use the 'channel for advertising'. On the contrary the bad news is that you can't specify the content, frequency or reach of the advertising.

Word of mouth is more effective than T.V, direct mail, and advertisements put together. Research has shown that it is 7000 more powerful than any medium of sale promotion. When making buying decisions, some customers take this into account more than the price- 'time' and 'hassle'.

The best example of word of mouth marketing is 'Hot-Mail'. In 1995 two young men from Silicon Valley, Sabeer Bhatia and Jack Smith, with the help of Draper Fischer Jurvetson (DFJ) a venture capitalist started the venture with a capital of $ 300,000 in seed money. As people found the free Email service, they would tell their family, friends, colleagues and acquaintances. Surprisingly within eighteen months Hotmail had twelve million subscribers. Incidentally Hotmail did not advertise. It was just word of mouth marketing of a great user experience.

It is necessary to communicate with the customers. If your customers buy your product and you don't communicate with them, you can't expect them to talk about your product or service to others. However, if you stimulate and ask them about the product, service and their experience, they will be enthusiastic to tell you and also others. Tell stories because people remember stories better than facts and figures. Good stories make people attentive; they participate, learn, remember and convey to others. Bank Manager or any staff member can tell the customers how small savings in recurring deposit or mutual fund has helped some customers in meeting the educational and marriage expenses of their children. Listening to such stories the prospect will be motivated to follow saving with the branch. He will not only do it for himself but will also communicate to others how he was motivated to save.

When Ford introduced the Thunderbolt, it sent invitations to executives offering them a free car drive for the day. Of the 15,000 who took advantage of the offer, 10 percent indicated that they would buy, whereas 84 percent said they would recommend it to their friends. This clearly shows how word of mouth marketing is a powerful tool in marketing.

It is valued by any business owner who desires to have loyal, satisfied customers to speak about their business. If you serve your customers well, they will be happy to spread a positive word about you. The ultimate aim is to convert customers to 'advocates' who praise and encourage others to bank with us.

Wow, word of mouth marketing is a great incentive to give excellent service.

Selling

Is the tip of the marketing iceberg? Selling can be defined as **"helping the customer to buy"**. The idea is to have a win- win situation for both the buyer and the seller. In such a situation both the parties are satisfied over the deal. If the seller sells a good product at a reasonable price to the buyer, he will come back again for a repeat purchase and also tell others about good qualities of the product. If a bad product sold and at a high cost, customer will be unhappy and he will never go back to the seller and bad mouth about the seller and the product to others. At the sales point it is generally an attitude of 'push' the product or service.

Selling requires excellent communication skills, to ask the right questions, to listen attentively, ability to generate interest and to provide relevant information to the satisfaction of the customer.

> **In short marketing can be defined as**
> **'pull' and selling as 'push'.**

The four activities to be used for increasing revenue generation are:

1. **Cross- selling**: Selling an additional product or service to an existing customer. For example customer is maintaining a savings bank account and if you sell him recurring deposit account, it is cross selling. It need not necessarily be a product of a partner or another company.

Why cross selling?

- To meet the varied and increasing needs of customers at one place.('enveloping' the customer)
- To retain the customers.
- To have an additional source of revenue to sustain growth in business and profit.
- To attract new customers.
- To maintain long relationship with customers.

2. **Up selling**: is the practice of offering customers more expensive items, upgrades, or other add-ons whereas cross-selling is selling an additional product to the existing customers.

3. **Increase share of wallet**: Refers to selling higher proportion of products and services to the existing customers. It can be done only by building trust with the customer. It is to increase the preference of the customer on our own product than the competitors.

4. **Reactivating customers**: if they are lost to competitor. One way to win back is to write a personalized letter. The letter should begin with something like this "we miss you! We want you back!" Explain the reasons why they should come back. The other way is by telephone. The message should be same as in the letter.

It was very interesting to read that Robert Craven (A first class international key note business speaker, author and consultant) has divided customers into, four simple to understand categories:

1. Strangers-the broader market, they don't know who I am.

2. Friends- prospective customers, they know who I am, but they haven't bought yet.
3. Lovers-current customers.
4. Ex-lovers – ex customers who have fallen out of love with us.

Internal Marketing

It is a simple fact that information is power. This is particularly a grey area for the banks and there is an urgent need to build strong internal marketing system. Most of the managers fail to pass on the information of new products and services to the employees. Lack of information leaves employees powerless and disinterested. Therefore, communication is important to deepen the knowledge of the employees. When employees understand the benefits of the product, external marketing becomes more effective. A better informed workforce can be a real source of competitive advantage. Experience has shown that in a branch only a few employees acquire the knowledge of the products and all the customers are directed to them. Most of the times it becomes difficult for those employees to satisfactorily explain the benefits of the product. Studies have, however, shown that 85% of companies did not have a budget for internal marketing and communications.

Internal customers don't constitute a single homogeneous group. Like external customers, they too have their own behavior patterns. One recommended form of segmentation is to divide employees into three groups.

• Supporters.
• Neutrals.
• Opponents.

Each group requires different marketing mix to achieve your marketing objective. It will be easy to handle the supporters and neutrals by explaining them in detail about the product and the services which will benefit the bank. In case of opponents more persuasive methods have to be applied for their attitudinal change.

Passing on the information to the employees is critical to the success of any marketing initiative. The employees are in direct contact with the customers in a variety of ways. They meet, greet and serve. They serve the customers,

1.   Face toface,
2.   Online,
3.   By telephone,
4.   And through correspondence.

Customer relationship depends on the attitude, knowledge, and loyalty of the employees. To motivate employees, it is necessary for the communication to flow upwards and downwards regularly. Internal marketing is a way to bind the two parties together with the shared values and goals.

Internal marketing helps to ignite employee's performance and delight customers.

What's the difference between a customer and a consumer?
A customer is a buyer, a purchaser or a shopper. A customer is someone who purchases from a shop, a website, a business and from some other customer. The difference between the customer and consumer is that while a customer buys a product or obtains a service, and the consumer consumes or uses it.

For example a customer has taken a loan for purchasing a home, his wife and children who are staying with him in that home are consumers. If you have enrolled in a course and the fees was paid by your father or someone else, then you are the consumer and father or other person who paid the fees are customers. In certain cases the customer and consumer can also be the same person. For example if you buy ice cream and eat it then you are the customer and also the consumer.

In bank marketing should be not only to serve customer but also to attract the consumer to buy our products. Experience has shown that in many cases the customer is banking with us and his working wife and children are maintaining their accounts in other banks. Since State Bank of India is a financial supermarket which can provide many products, the consumers should be brought into its fold. This could happen only if the customer is given an extremely good customer service and he becomes an evangelist for word of mouth marketing to advocate his folks to bank with us. Know your customer (KYC) norms also provide a detailed profile of the customer, from which leads could be obtained to follow up with his family members to buy our products and services. Enrolling consumers into customers will be less cost effective than a prospect.

What is a brand? The definition of a brand is Identification of a business product, services and organization through a combination of name, symbol, design and colors. It distinguishes a business among its competitors. (Definition from web). We identify a company through its products, customer care and by its logo or symbol. The symbol refers to the customer value. For example State Bank of India's symbol of circle with a key hole represents that the country's largest bank serves the smallest man. The symbol of State Bank of

India stands for its value and the common man identifies it with stability, safety, reliability and is attracted towards it.

Brand loyalty

It occurs due to deep seated commitment, emotional attachment, customer service and taste. This is often seen in buying of consumer products like tomato- sauce, toothpaste, soaps and automobiles. Most of the sauces available in the market contain the same ingredients like tomatoes, sugar and salt but we prefer to buy a particular sauce repeatedly over the years because of its taste. We have never tried to taste the other sauces because of the compelling taste of that particular brand. Same thing happens to many of us in our buying decisions for toothpaste and soaps. Recently to my surprise my friend purchased a new Maruthi-Alto car after disposing her old Maruthi-800 though I had advised her to go for a new brand. She cheerfully explained to me that for the last 10 years the use of Maruthi-800 had given her least botheration for maintenance which shows that she was emotionally and rationally attached to the brand. Who said familiarity (always) breeds contempt.

Brand Equity: It is the value of a brand built over a period of time. This includes brands with a fair degree of consumer awareness. The buyers select them over others. The brands are one of the most powerful assets the company has. The brand name carries high credibility and it offers companies some defense against fierce competition. A powerful brand has high brand equity. A brand with strong brand equity is a valuable asset of the company. Brand equity is an intangible asset that depends on associations made with the consumer. The term brand equity is used to describe both the value of the brand and the brand's component values.

10

TELEPHONE HUG

Telephone is an indispensable part of our lifestyle. The most compelling need today is telephone after roti (bread), kapda (cloth), makan (dwelling). India is the fastest growing telecom market, with the lowest mobile tariffs in the world. The cell phone has brought an unprecedented revolution in communication. It has changed our social and family life. We are not personally visiting our brothers, sisters and customers. We just connect to them by phone. Most of the things are done on phone right from banking, buying air ticket, paying our bills and even filing a complaint with the police.

Of course speaking to siblings and friends is quite different from speaking to customers. Banks and other organizations generally consider speaking on the phone by their employees is a matter of routine. In banks the telephone is mostly picked up by the subordinate staff or by the official/clerk in the proximity. This staff doesn't understand the impact of their talk on the customer because hardly any training was provided to the employees on telephone communication skills. We should remember that to the customer at the other end, whoever speaks on the phone is the representative of the bank. Good telephone communication skills benefit your bank; create your image over the phone. Effective communication on telephone helps us to understand the needs and views of the customer. Our skills in listening, promptly attending to customer needs will help us to build lasting customer relationship. The telephone is the most powerful link with the customer. Telephone is the best, cheapest and most effective tool for building rapport, customer service, customer loyalty, customer retention and selling various products of the bank. This also includes cross selling and up selling. Many banks spend plenty of time and money on training their employees to excel in face to face communication with the customer ignoring to groom them on telephone etiquette. Banks should train employees to hone their telephone communication skills so that they can provide a friendly, effective service to customers as well as contributing to achieve the business targets. The training should enable employees deliver customer delight at every contact.

Branch Manager must have at least 100 telephone numbers of his customers on his cell phone.

Accountant/ Field Officers must have telephone numbers of valuable customers on their cell phones.

In every account the column of phone number should invariably be filled up.

Sometimes we are shocked to call bank whose employees have answered the phone with a simple "hello".

To make sure we have reached the right place, we ask "is it happy bank". The unenthusiastic reply is "yes happy bank".

"I need to speak to your accountant". Please hold. I am on hold for 2 minutes without any response, the line gets disconnected. On calling again the phone gives an engage beep. To our horror after trying several times the same person lifts the phone and when reminded he makes attempts to get the accountant to the phone. Let's examine how the call was treated.

1. In the first place the person who received my call did not identify himself.
2. No courtesy offered like greeting the customer.
3. He did not tell the name of the bank making me uncertain about the place of landing.
4. He made me a faceless person. He did not ask my name.
5. He kept me on hold without intimating the response of the person whom I wanted to contact.
6. I had to try several times to contact the person feeling frustrated and disgusted in dealing with such unprofessional bank.

Tips for answering the call,

1. Answer the call before the third ring.
2. Before picking up the phone, rid your mouth of chewing gum, candy, pan because the receiver amplifies your noshing.
3. Receive the call with a standard professional greeting depending on the time of the day, like good morning, good afternoon and well after noon, good evening.
4. Mention your name, organization slowly and clearly, don't haste. This will make the customer comfortable because he will know that he has landed at the proper place and to whom he is speaking.
   Example,

"good morning sir/Maam, State bank of India, Hussain; can I help you?

5. Try to smile, the caller will appreciate. The customer on the other end will not be able to see the person smiling but they can hear it in the tone of the voice (smile relaxes the muscles and this will have a similar effect on the voice tone). Smile in your voice will present you as a positive and helpful person.

6. Always use "please" or "Thank you" and try to be very polite and courteous.
Remember that you are representing your bank. Using courteous phrases are essentially in conveying professional approach.

7. Ask the caller's name if you are not able to recognize his voice. "May I know your name please"?

8. Then use the name during conversation by adding the prefix "sir" or "maam" as the case may be.

9. Listen carefully without interrupting, use words like "I see", "sir/ma am", so that the caller feel that you are interested in listening him.

10. Don't shuffle papers while speaking over phone.

11. If the customer wants to give a complaint/suggestion on your products or service, give him/her your mailing address, email address and fax number.

12. If the caller has reached a wrong number, be courteous. Don't bang the phone since you have already told your organization name after receiving the call, say wrong number and slowly keep the receiver.

13. Don't make a habit of receiving personal call at office or if received by chance received, try to be brief.

14. Thank the caller for calling. Say "thanks for calling".

15. When the named employee is not available, tell the caller, right now the person you want to speak is not available, and will you leave a message. Can I help you?

16. When you transfer a call, please inform the caller that his call is being transferred to the person concerned or to the person whom he wants to speak.

17. Educate the customers to mention phone number on all vouchers (debit & credit), account opening form, and any representation so that he can be easily contacted.

18. Put a notice in the banking hall advising the customers to update their phone numbers with the bank. The customers are frequently changing the phone numbers resulting in difficulty in contacting them.

Handling irate or impatient callers:

1. Stay calm and be polite.

2. Don't haste and get angry.

3. Listen carefully and try to resolve the problem.

4. If not able to provide information which a customer needs instantly or solve the problem, take the caller contact number and assure to get back to him.

5. Make sure to contact him. The customer should not lose trust in you as service provider. If you promptly contact the customer he will feel you are sincere and committed to resolve his problem.

6. Most of the times the irate customer wants to speak to the manager to narrate his problem so pass on the call to the manager.

Taking messages,

1. Keep a telephone message slip when you answer the phone.
2. Ask the caller name (full name). If you jot down just Sharma, the recipient may know many Sharmas. He will not be able to know which Sharma had telephoned. Take the full name.
3. Note caller's phone number including extension number.
4. Ask the caller his message. Repeat the message to the caller.
5. Place the message on the called person's table.

Telephone message note pads should be distributed to all the staff members so that the can readily use it in the following format.

TELEPHONE MESSAGE

For _____

From _____

Tel _____Extn _____

Message:

Action required: Please call back

Voicemail greeting,

1. Record in your own voice. If it is recorded in some one else's voice the customer will lose the personal touch.
2. Write the message, practice it and then record it.
3. Include in your greeting your name and bank name so that the customer knows that he has reached the right place.
4. If you are on long leave then include the phone number and name of the other person who could be contacted.

Checking message box and returning calls,

1. Check the message box daily and return the calls. Callers will feel great that you care for them.
2. After calling the caller delete the message, keep your call box clean and provide space for new calls.

Phrases to memorized and used frequently,

1. It was so nice talking to you.
2. Thank you for calling.
3. Please be in touch with us.
4. Can I help you?
5. Have a good day.
6. I am sorry to keep you waiting.

Phrases not to be used,

1. How do I know?
2. No, not possible.

3. Don't disturb, I am busy.
4. We can't do it.
5. "Are you following what I am saying"?

Customer service through phone: On a particular day my senior assistant informed me that the cheque of the customer will be returned as the balance was insufficient. I asked her to immediately dial the customer over his cell phone as the number was available on the screen. The phone was picked by his wife and informed us that her husband had forgotten the cell phone at home. Then immediately his office phone was dialed but again it was informed that he had gone to canteen for a cup of tea. As our extension counter was located in their office we asked our messenger to contact him and inform about the insufficient balance. As soon as the customer was informed of insufficient balance he immediately paid the amount and the cheque was cleared. This saved the honour of the customer and penalty for insufficient balance for cheque return. The customer was very delighted for our persuasive way of locating and informing him. In one of our cross selling campaign, he obliged the employee by buying a product her. This clearly shows that appropriate use of telephone has helped us in customer delight and also building trust. On several occasions our branch contacted the customers to inform them about insufficient balances in their accounts, repayment of loans, conveying greetings on birthday, marriage anniversary, on their promotion and on many more such happy occasions. Thanks to Mrs. Sujatha (our employee) for delighting the customer.

Cell phone etiquette:

Cell phone is the most important tool for all of us. It has brought a revolution in telephone communication. The desk top phone has lost much of its utility after the arrival of the cell phone. Try to achieve some standards in cell phone etiquette to be appreciated by your customers, callers and employees.

Ring tones- Set the ring tone at a low level with a tune that is gentle, soft and not annoying. Ring tones for the caller should be a standard tone not filmy song, jazz or religious hymns.

Focus on the call- When the call comes through stop other activities like typing, reading, handling key board and focus on the call. Listen and give full attention to the call. The goal is to communicate with the customer in the most effective manner. Speak softly and be polite.

While attending other customer: When the call comes through while attending to other customer say "excuse me" and attend the call. Try to be focused and brief. Don't repeat what the customer said, to protect the confidentiality of the conversation. Avoid personal calls in front of customers. All personal calls should be after office hours.

If you are driving; never talk while driving. It is unlawful and risky to talk while driving. If necessary, pull over the car on the side and then speak.

Turn it off – In meetings turn it off or keep it on silent, vibration mode. While attending the call leave the room to ensure privacy and not to disturb others.

Check the received calls log and do the courtesy of calling back. This will help us make a good and professional impression on the customer.

Save the cell phone number of the customer – so that next time he telephones you can wish him by name. Instant recognition will work like magic on the customer.

Tips for calling the customer,

1. Don't call the customer before 8 a.m and not after 9 p.m.
2. Ask the person whether you can talk now. This will help to decide his option; sometimes the customer may be busy.
3. Try to be brief, keep the conversation short and to the point.
4. Make the customers feel they are talking to a friend. Be polite, be concerned, assure them, praise them; do anything that makes them trust and trust goes a long way in customer relation.
5. Try to accomplish something during these calls like building relationship, feed back, cross selling and up selling.
6. Say something which interests them. They may be more interested to know the latest interest rates, new bank products, about saving schemes, mutual funds and insurance.
7. Contact at least some customers daily and speak to them about our products and services. It is difficult to visit customers because of traffic jams and distance so visit them by phone.
8. While closing the call, briefly wrap up the conversation. Repeat the whole conversation, greet them and say thank you for your business or just simply say thank you.

SMS etiquette,

1.   Don't send message in capital letters.
2.   Try to be brief but meaningful.
3.   No code language should be used like 4 u (for you), NE (any), HAND (have a nice day), because a customer above 50 years old may not understand your message.
4.   Check the time. If you are sending to a person abroad see that it doesn't disturb his sleep.
5.   Avoid unnecessary spaces in the message. This will be included in the word count by your telephone operator.
6.   Be prompt and courteous; reply the messages. The sender will be happy to receive your acknowledgement. Let the sender know that you care.
7.   Send messages to customers in conveying your happy wishes and to share their happiness and sometimes their grief.
8.   If your message is not acknowledged do not repeatedly send SMS, have patience.
9.   Excellent messages received from customers, share it with your employees.
10.   Don't type messages while driving; it is unlawful in some countries.

Proper telephone etiquette will certainly make a positive impression on your customers.

11

COMPLAINTS

Why complaints happen? We give excellent service but customers still complain. We all love to listen to compliments and not complaints. We become defensive and look at the complainants with contempt. Customer complaints are never easy to hear. We fail to realize that when the service or product is below expectations of the customer, complaint happens. A complaint can be defined as "an expression of dissatisfaction made to an organization, related to its products, or the complaints handling process itself, where a response or resolution is explicitly or implicitly expected". ISO 1002:2004.

Complaint could be a whisper or it could be a scream. Customers have lot of expectations from the banks. They come to the bank expecting to be recognized, to be attended and conclude transactions within a short time. But they find a long queue and it takes a long time to complete the transaction. The customers are highly disappointed and they are a dissatisfied lot. Most of the dissatisfied customers may not complain but may change the bank if the competitor bank provides better service. Today customers are more knowledgeable about their rights and would often use their option to complain.

It is interesting to note the difference in expectation of customer service from rural, semi urban, urban and metro customers. Out of all these customers the urban and metro customer are more likely to complain. They have more options and are highly technology savvy. The moment they experience deficiency in service they complain since they have access to the internet and they immediately lodge complaint on the internet site of the bank.

To get the feel about your customer service, take a walk in your premises in the morning before arrival of the customers to check the amenities, cleanliness and staff attendance. Remember customer is always in a hurry, he/she doesn't want to spend more than five minutes in your bank. This is the threshold of customer patience. If he/she is not able to get service within anticipated time of five minutes he/she develops a grouse against the bank which will reflect in the customer transaction. The more the customer is annoyed the thinner becomes the transaction.

There are many things which may lead to a customer complaint:

1. Counters not opened on time.
2. There is no one to handle transaction.
3. Pensions not credited to their account.
4. Wrong debits.
5. Transaction not clear.
6. Delay in cheque collection.
7. Soiled notes.
8. Long queue.
9. Wrong interest calculation.
10. Delay in sanctioning loan.
11. No response on telephone.
12. Rude behavior.
13. No proper amenities.

14. No reply to letters.
15. And many more.

Why complaint handling is important?

If complaint is resolved to the satisfaction of the complainant, loyalty of the customer improves and experience shows that these customers frequent the banks for more business. Complaint handling is important to fix the problem. The customer is informed that it has been fixed to gain his goodwill. Positive feelings are generated in those customers whose problems have been settled politely and speedily. British Airways believe that a "right first attitude" and effective complaint handling lead to maximum customer satisfaction and loyalty. If you deal with a customer complaint sincerely and helpfully, your efforts will be appreciated, the customer will feel happy and valued. The data shows that you can get back 95 percent customers if their complaint is resolved timely and satisfactorily. Careful complaint management can save unwanted costs and improve profits. Negative word of mouth publicity from dissatisfied customers will necessitate additional investment in publicity to counter it. The complaint provides us an opportunity to adjust, to rectify the problem and restores trust. From the data available, we find that only a fraction of the customers make compliant and most of the dissatisfied customers don't complain. These non complaining customers are skeptical about the services, products and simply switch over to the other bank and also pass on critical comments about your Bank to others. Negative word of mouth publicity from unsatisfied customers will do more harm to the bank.

Complaint will help in improving service and products. Complaint should not be considered as criticism but it is to be considered as a constructive idea to improve service, behavior, product deficiencies and product information. McDonalds says complaints from customers are precious pieces of information. When used properly complaints can help us fine tune our business and help us meet customer needs. The unsatisfied customers will tell us how to do our job better and alert us against further deterioration of our service. They will also bring out the deficiencies in our products that need improvement. Banks can learn to rectify them and turn unhappy, frustrated customers into happy and loyal ones. Customers who have a problem successfully solved will be more loyal than the customer who had never complained.

Complaint should not be defended; it will further annoy the complainant. A systematic effective innovative method of complaint handling mechanism will assuage the feeling of the complainant. Remember an unsatisfied customer is a ripe target for the competitor. So be friendly with complainants, it will:

- Help us in improving service and product.
- Lead to Better understanding of customer needs.
- Increase customer loyalty.
- Generates more referrals through word of mouth marketing by satisfied customers.
- Improve business.
- Help us in repeat business.
- Help us to avoid recurrence of the mistake.
- Help turn frustrated customers into loyal customers and gain an advantage over competitors.

It is evident that a well executed complaint handling mechanism will pay off. The urgency and the seriousness in handling the complaint will make the customer happy and will go a long way in building trust and loyalty. Quick response is vital in resolving complaints. If complaint handling system is poor, it will further alienate the customer, resulting in lower purchase rate. The complaint handling should be transparent, independent and objective.

Customer retention strategy: no business can afford to lose customers. In today's competitive world customer has more choice than they ever had. So the banks need to be more vigilant in retaining customer. It cost eight times more to court a new customer than to retain the existing one. A dissatisfied customer also spends money to make a phone call, to lodge a complaint, go to banking ombudsman and most importantly passes through an agonizing experience which he had to endure through out. For example, a customer had issued cheque to electricity department towards payment of his monthly electric consumption bill and due to oversight it was not cleared. As a result, his electricity was disconnected for non payment of the bill. The customer had to undergo the pangs of living without electricity for a day or two till the bank takes notice of the mistake. Customer is highly enraged and takes up the matter with the controllers and if not resolved then will approach the banking ombudsman. These are the hidden costs of the complaint which the customer incurs by approaching different fora to redress the customer's grievances. The controllers who are innovative and geared for excellent customer service will go an extra mile to cover the cost.

How to identify salient complainants, Studies have shown that 96% of the unhappy customers don't complain they simply switch to the competitors. There are many ways to encourage these customers to speak about their unhappiness. Some are listed below,

Meet regularly customers in the banking hall and seek their opinion. Solve their problem immediately with a smile.

Analyze how complaints can be prevented.

Encourage employees to listen to customer complaints and resolve them.

Train the front line staff to handle complaints, teach the front line employees to receive complaints as gifts and train them:

1. To listen,
2. To fix the problem,
3. To restore customer confidence,
4. And to regain goodwill.

When the employee follows the above cordial relationship between the employee and customer will develop. The employee and the customer will both feel valued. Research by Baines and Co. reveals that 68% of existing customers switch to the competitors because no one keeps in touch with them.

Perdue is the number one brand of premium fresh chicken in eastern USA.

If a customer complains to Perdue then it takes the following action, The customer:

- Is mailed a letter of apology.
- Is asked to fill out a questionnaire with regard to the problem.
- Is called by a corporate VP.
- Is given a coupon for a free chicken.

With the above action the complainant customer turns an evangelist for the company and sing praises before others.

Learn from the complaint; it is an opportunity to learn from complaints. It was something that was missing in your product or service that was brought to your notice. This should help you to re-examine and improve. Don't hide the complaints, bring it to the knowledge of colleagues and higher up so that remedial measures could be initiated. Review the complaints in the monthly staff meetings. Ensure remedial measures to avoid reoccurrence. If it is beyond your capacity to rectify then pass it on to your controllers. This will help the corporate to capture the complaint data on a wider scale from different locations to understand the emotion of the customer. The corporate office will set in motion to analyze the root causes and to develop and improve products and services for better market orientation.

Language; is the most important tool in communicating and cooling the ruffled feelings of the customer. The way the customer complaints are handled indicates how serious the manager is in solving customer complaints. Handling customer complaint is a difficult communication task. This requires particular skills when dealing with customers who are not satisfied with particular product or service. Positive language has the power to take control of the situation. It reassures the complainant that a fair treatment is being extended to the customer. Managers who need to succeed in their careers should remember that effective communication skills, both oral and written, are absolutely necessary. Managers who want to please and retain the customer have to effectively and efficiently communicate. Managers possessing effective communication skills can help enhance customer retention, delight and credibility.

The sentences which are to be used to pacify the customers are, We are very sorry for the inconvenience,

We would like to apologize,

Thank you for bringing this problem to our notice,

I am delighted to inform you that your complaint has been dealt with, I am happy to tell you,

Body language; they say 'a picture paints a thousand words', and the same can be said of our gestures. In a charged up atmosphere only 5 percent is verbal communication and the rest is body language. If the customer is standing you should also stand and talk. First bring yourself to the level of customer. Then politely ask the customer to sit and lean forward to listen so as to give an impression that you are actively listening. While listening don't stand with hands on hips (it means aggression), arms crossed on chest, (this shows you are defensive), rubbing nose (signifies rejection and doubt), rubbing eyes (means doubt and disbelief), hands clasped back (indicates anger), open arms shows sincerity, patting hair means lack of confidence and quickly tilted head means interest. Customers would freely approach manager who is smiling with his arms on his side, hands open, courteous and polite.

Whenever you receive a complaint make sure to take the phone number and e mail address of the customer so that the customer can be easily contacted. If the address is not available then it will be difficult for you to contact and it will send wrong signals to the customer. You may waste time in searching for the address.

Make it easy for customers to complain;

- All the banks have installed customer complaints and suggestion boxes in their branches.
- The names and phone numbers of their controllers are displayed at prominent places in the branches.
- The phone number and address of the banking ombudsman is also displayed in the branches.

More novel ways of customer participation are adopted by foreign entities,

- British Airways installed "video point" booths in Heathrow airport in London so that travelers can tape their comments on arrival.
- The Toronto Dominion Bank, the second largest bank of Canada offered customers a five dollar bill if they waited for more than five minutes in line.
- Maine savings bank in Portland offers its patrons one dollar for every letter they write suggesting ways to improve customer service. The bank averages more than 500 letters a year from customers, who might otherwise have kept their ideas to themselves.

According to a recent study conducted by Mckinsey & Co the customers of banks in India are the most satisfied customers in Asia. However the RBI reports an increase in complaints particularly against public sector banks.

The maximum number of complaints against public sector banks is for transaction in deposit accounts, for private and foreign banks, related to credit cards. It also includes complaints on remittances and general customer service.

The CEO of Indian banks' association attributes the rise in customer complaints to rising business volumes. There cannot be 100% customer satisfaction with a huge volume of transaction as a result of economic growth. Despite your best efforts there will be some customers who cannot be made happy. Incidentally the address and phone numbers of the banking ombudsman is mandatory to be displayed at prominent positions in public sector banks. As such some of the customers directly complain to the banking ombudsman before bringing it to the notice of the branch manager or the senior officials of the bank. Obviously in these days of intense competition to attract and retain customers no branch manager more particularly of public sector bank would take the risk of annoying the customer. The customers of public sector banks are not from the upper segment of the society and consist mostly of lower middle class households and pensioners. The minimum balance required in public sector bank is Rs.500 for a non cheque book account compared to minimum balance of Rs.10, 000 in private and foreign banks. There are lakhs of no frill accounts without any balance. However the manager of public sector bank is more careful in handling his customers as the management of public sector banks treats all the customers on equal footing unlike their counter parts in private and foreign banks.

In these days of internet and blogging bad customer service will get noticed on the web. There are many blogs of bad customer service on the internet and many thousands will read these. There are as on now 8, 10, 00,000 internet users in India. Study shows that as many as 10, 000 people will read a blog and the effect of bad customer service could be disastrous. These effects of blogging are more from younger customers as they are more adventurous. They could indulge in writing a blog conveying displeasure without even informing the concerned bank about the bad experience.

Regular review of complaints; will gives us an indication of our deficiencies in service delivery. It will help us to identify the areas for improvement. Watch out for the trends in complaint. Review the complaints regularly in staff meetings and seek assistance and suggestion from employees to improve service and reduce complaints. Refer the records to see how quickly the earlier complaints were handled.

Tips for complaint handling,

- Acknowledge the complaint promptly.
- Take all complaints seriously.
- Give equal treatment to all customers.
- Treat complainants with respect, sensitivity and courtesy.
- Attend and solve complaints urgently.
- Contact the complainant immediately and assure to resolve the complaint.
- If it takes time to resolve the complaint be in touch with the complainant.
- The procedure should be fast, fair, convenient and confidential.
- Listen carefully to the complainant.
- Act quickly.
- Console the customer and offer apology.
- Handle complaint timely and correctly.
- Personally thank them for bringing complaint to your attention.

Internet accessibility; Internet has given to customers a quick easy way to vent their feelings. Courtesy alone doesn't help in restricting the customer from complaining in this e-customer age. The latest technology in transacting the business is what the customer expects. E customers are very demanding. Identify their expectations and respond to their needs. Any slip in handling the technology will result in customer complaint. Most of them make use of all the facilities provided to them through internet banking. They communicate through the internet for cheque book, for term deposit and request for many more services. If there is delay in delivery of products and services requested by them through internet they will feel frustrated. The delays in carrying out their requests often end up in lodging complaint with the higher ups. The staff needs to be aware of the products and services available on the core banking platform and internet to satisfy these customers.

Some customers are complaining type; they love to complain now and then. They are never satisfied. Complaints could be dangerous and sometimes they could tarnish your image.

Remember if the complaint is not handled properly customer is going to walk away and will never come back.

> **If the complaint is handled properly then
> you create goodwill, customer loyalty
> and an evangelist for your bank.**

SUCCESSFUL MEETINGS

Nobody can avoid death, taxes and meetings. Every one of us complains about meetings, there are too many. Some are tiring and don't work. Nay we have fewer options to avoid meetings. But some meetings are useful, effective and productive. Meetings are important because these are the fora for communication within the team or between a team and other team to achieve organizational goals. The meeting also helps us to know what is happening in the organization. Meeting helps to exchange ideas with colleagues, listen to their problems, and agree on actions and sometimes receive good advice to solve problems. Meetings are necessary to align the group to move in a planned and strategic manner. Communication, planning and aligning are essentials of the meeting. The purpose of the meeting is to produce results and not just to make minor adjustments.

Significantly regular staff meetings will help to reinforce desired attitudes and motivate them to deliver excellent customer service. During the meetings employees will learn finer points from their colleagues which can improve their performance. The meetings will help the manager to focus on improving service quality and significantly increasing customer loyalty while simultaneously boosting sales and enhancing profitability.

When our performance figures are low we are scared to attend meetings because of the fear that the boss may take us to task in the presence of other colleagues. In such situations we keep a low profile and sit with anxiety to face our turn. On the contrary, when our figures are high we dominate the meetings.

In the branch too we hold meetings like monthly staff meeting, customer service committee meeting, customer relations programmes and many such meetings. To make such meetings successful, appropriate planning has to be made so as to have the desired results. You and your staff will be facing the same challenging and demanding circumstances. It is important to listen and take the feedback from the participants for the desired results. The information you receive in the meeting will make you more confident in dealing with the problems. It is vital to encourage the active participation of every member and make them contribute ideas.

Three sets of participants; a well run meeting has a leader, recorder and active members.

Leader- is the person who sets the agenda, selects and invites participants. Recorder- is entrusted with the task of recording the minutes of the meeting. Participants- Those who are invited, provide feedback and contribute ideas.

To save time one should prioritize the agenda, first things first and make sure to start the meeting on time.

Tips for effective meetings,

1. Advise date and time of meeting.
2. Define the purpose of the meeting.
3. Set objectives for the meeting.
4. Prepare agenda with the help of the employees.
5. Distribute the agenda in advance.
6. Choose an appropriate and convenient time.
7. Arrange sitting in a circle.
8. Decide action plan.
9. Punctuality is a must. It is bad manners to keep people waiting.
10. Make it a point to be brief but clear and allow others to participate

11. Review the minutes of the earlier meeting.
12. Don't end meeting abruptly.
13. Ask the participants to keep the mobiles on silent mode or switch the mobiles.
14. Never interrupt any one.
15. Convey thanks at the end of meeting

Agenda: The first and foremost thing is preparing the agenda and then circulate it to the participants for a meaningful discussion. This will help the participants to come prepared.

Snacks in the meeting: Provide healthy food and beverages in the meeting like prepackaged fruit cups and dried fruits. Serve beverages like 100 percent vegetable, fruit juice and coffee or tea. Remember employees are attending meeting after a full days tiring work so you should take care in arranging snacks and beverages which should be lip smacking. The eatables will help relax, rejuvenate and encourage them to participate more enthusiastically. Caffeine plays an important role in keeping the mind alert. Foliate in vitamin B, found in orange juice is said to improve alertness. Be generous in providing nutritious and delicious snacks. If you serve routine tea and biscuits then it will be a dull and drab meeting. If you want your meeting to be successful, lively, energetic and proactive, serve the best snacks. In customer meetings remember to ask invitees of any special dietary requirements. Some of them may be diabetics and some will be strict vegetarians who avoid eggs in cakes, garlic and onions in pizzas. This will save you from embarrassment for not serving proper snacks. But be generous in providing nutritious and delicious snacks.

Control your own behavior; this is vital in all meetings. Some of the participants may have unresolved issues which affect their attitudes and commitment. They may flare up with the slightest provocation. This will make your job difficult to handle. But if you stay calm and do not overreact to the situation it will subside on its own. Always talk politely and emphasize the objective of the meeting. Sit straight and place your feet flat. Don't yawn and whisper to the person sitting next. Listen more than talking. Don't try to dominate in the meeting. It is worth to listen both negative and positive feedback. Make it a point to be brief, clear and allow others to participate. If you find that on some contentious issues tempers flare up, step in to defuse the tension. Try to be non-aligned, without putting your weight behind any one of the groups.

Invite right people to the meeting; for purposeful meetings right type of people should be invited. For example in staff meetings only those designated to attend the meeting should be invited. There are several other types of meetings like traders, farmers, small scale industry owners, personal segment and high valued customers, etc. In a farmers meet if you invite small scale industries owners it will become difficult for the latter group to participate. The needs, wants and views of each segment will be different. Customers should be segmented so that you can avoid huge wastage of time for the participants by inviting unconcerned people. Plan carefully before inviting the people for the meeting. It is important to invite the right mix of people. Try to limit the number of people so that all the concerned get a chance to put forward their views.

Contact details; provide your or any one of your assistants contact details on the invitation so that people can contact in case of emergency. If they express their inability to attend don't get upset, politely request them to make it convenient for the next meeting.

Don't allow one person to dominate; some participants dominate the meeting and frequently interrupt others. It is of course bad manners and discourteous to interrupt others. The chair should take care to restrain them from interrupting others. As a rule allow only one person to talk and request the other persons to calmly listen. Some people are vociferous and hijack the meetings. Look around to see if some one wants to speak by raising their hands. Don't allow unnecessary and unrelated issues. When and if people enter into side conversations which disturb the concentration of other participants discourage it.

Customer meetings – is a great opportunity to meet them and understand their concerns. Feedback from these meetings can be a valuable source in understanding and appreciating the views of our customers on our products and services. Customers will also suggest to us how to streamline our working for the mutual benefit. It is a face to face meeting to discuss the problems and find solutions. These meetings are the best source for the employees and customers to communicate in a friendly manner. The meeting helps the bank to improve its image and firmly convey to the customer that the bank is eager to respond and adapt to their needs. The customer meet is an incredible way to make the customer feel valued and an opportunity for the bank to take care of their needs. The banks, in these meetings, can also educate the customer about the operations of new technology products and arrange for cross selling products and services. In these meetings some of the deserving customers and their wards can also be felicitated for their achievements.

Customers in the upper end of the market tend to keep a low profile and rarely attend such meetings. In such a scenario individual personalized meetings may be conducted.

Seating arrangement in customer meeting: Good etiquette is of paramount importance in arranging seating for the customers. We spend a lot of time in planning meeting, sending invitations, choosing the snacks, arranging the audio visual aids, decorating the hall, but hardly pay any attention to the seating arrangement. Often the customers are very sensitive about the way they are offered seats. Some would like to sit nearer to the chair in front rows as they deem it as a prestige. It is preferable to have a circular pattern. For good interaction and better distribution of ideas it is easier when customers seat in a circular pattern. There will not be any power centers and they will all feel equally valued. Circular arrangements will foster camaraderie and there will be free flow of ideas. Our society is feudal by nature and any mismatch in seating arrangement of our customers will create unpleasantness. Seating arrangement should not be left to chance because where the participants sit can actually influence the overall effectiveness of the meeting. It should be well planned and executed to the satisfaction of all.

Larger groups: The most commonly used style of seating is class room type. In this type of seating the manager and special invitee most probably the head office functionaries will sit opposite facing the audience. This will be a passive session in the starting where the special invitee will present his ideas followed by an interactive session.

Inviting boss in customer meetings: In some of our customer meetings we invite our controllers. Sometimes they turn up late making the customers wait. It is bad manners to keep customers waiting. The moment they arrive we forget our customers and follow the boss. We arrange bouquets and garland him ignoring the customers. No doubt our boss deserves special treatment because he is one of the most important variables in our job. Our boss should also understand that for all of us it is the customer who is first. No doubt it is difficult to balance but be chivalrous and manage the situation delighting both the customer and the boss.

Negative customers: Some customers have a negative approach for everything and anything. They take pleasure in criticizing. Don't ignore them. Listen patiently and ask them what they actually want. If it is reasonable look into it for implementation. Then after implementation confront them and tell that their suggestion was accepted and implemented. This way you can turn them from negative to neutral or positive customers.

Language: Customer meeting undoubtedly will be held in the language which they understand. In some situations our senior executives do not know the local language, and it is advisable to arrange a translator for the convenience of the customer. Language helps us to build trust with the customer.

The chairperson's role: The manager of the branch mostly chairs the meetings. He should manage the meeting with a polite countenance without throwing his weight around every discussion. His job is to control and direct the meeting. He should encourage active participation and maintain neutrality. He should address the customers with name and add suffix sir, ma am, doctor or professor. Ask the participants to keep the mobiles on silent mode or switch them off. Attentiveness and clear communication is the key to successful meeting. The most important point is to achieve the objective.

To organize a customer meet: The first and foremost is to make two teams and delegate the responsibilities. Employees will feel valued if they are involved.

Red team – to prepare the venue, guest lists, sending invitation and contacting customers.

Yellow team- receives the guest, arrange snacks and communicate with them.

Prepare the venue:

- Arrange the layout.
- Connect audio visuals and check it.
- Check the refreshments.
- Place the name plates, note books, pens and paper.
- Technical people like electrician should be on hand.

Receive the customers: It is very important that the guests are received enthusiastically. We are all well aware the power of the first impression and this applies just as much for meeting as any other situations in life. Receive each customer with a short but meaningful 'Thank you for coming', smile and shake hand. Your reception will set the positive tone of the meeting.

Building relationship:

- Smile- it is a non verbal friendly gesture and a welcome sign for the customers to interact.
- Make eye contact. Looking directly into the eye is the first step in making positive impressions.
- Shake hands- warm enthusiastic hand shake is the most important professional greeting.
- Appearance, looking good is all that important
- Introduce your staff.
- Make the customers feel valued.

- Show them you respect colleagues and your staff.
- Make the customers feel valued.
- If some one arrives late, they should be greeted and shown where to sit.
- Above all be sincere.

Humour is essential: A good sense of humor is essential to make the meeting lively. No doubt humor stimulates creativity, lively atmosphere and productivity but care should be taken not to upset the customers. It is better to direct humor towards you than towards others. We enjoy witty and humorous people. Wit and humor lubricate the channel of communication. Humor captivates the attention of the participants. Spice the meeting with humor to keep the meeting lively.

Smart customers- Some customer may crack a joke so as to become popular and make fun about us. Don't take it as an offence. Sometimes such jokes relax the participants. You can deal by saying that "yes there is a point in what he said". Then try to analyze it and the person will be careful in attempting another joke on us.

Encourage participation: it is about helping others to voice their feelings. It is to give other people respect and space they deserve. Some customers will be extrovert and they will dominate the meeting without much substance.

Handling difficult situations:

- Personalize the discussion by using the customer's name.

- Listen, stay calm, and show that you care and that you will do best to solve the problem.
- Ask questions; try to put in his own words so that the customer understands that you understood.
- If you are not able to reply take the help of some of your colleagues to reply.
- Ask politely what should be done.
- Take notes so that customer feels, his grievances is noted for action.
- If you think the problem cannot be solved, don't say 'no'. Explain why it cannot be done.
- Avoid over promise and under delivery, never promise more than you can deliver.
- Where appropriate, remind them of previous occasions, when you have solved their problems.
- Remaining calm will defuse tense/charged situations.
- Don't interrupt the customer. Let him vent his feelings to get it off his chest.
- Jointly develop a solution.
- Ask for alternatives.

Wrap up the meeting: Have a question and answer session at the end of the meeting. Politely answer the questions without showing any haste. Conducting professional, effective and interesting meetings will keep you ahead of your competitors.

Happy ending: Ensure that the staff efforts are recognized in conducting the meeting. Praise their efforts. Praising will work wonders for the persons self esteem. Profusely thank customers for attending the meeting. Make sure that the meeting has a happy ending and all the customers feel satisfied and delighted. Walk up to the entrance to say good bye to the customers.

After the meeting:

Meetings give us a huge feedback on the quality of service and products we offer. If we fail to go through the feedback, all the effort that has gone into making the meeting effective and interesting will be wasted. We procrastinate to review the meetings due to every day pressures.

It is important for the action agreed upon in the meeting to be attended to build trust and long term relationship with the customer.

TIPS TO HUG

1. Smile
2. Greet.
3. Smile.
4. Greet the customer by name (if you know the name).
5. Eye contact (not too long with women)
6. Firm shake hand. (not with ladies unless they offer).
7. Wear identity card.
8. Answer phone within 3 rings.
9. Offer seat to customers.
10. Enquire about their children.
11. Listen to the customers.
12. Encourage employees to chat with the customers.
13. Open the doors before time.
14. Keep news papers and magazines in the customer area.
15. Put light music in the branch.
16. Put fragrance sticks or spray air freshener.
17. Just get around and talk to your customers.
18. Offer chocolates to the accompanying children.
19. Regularly telephone customers.
20. Arrange for immediate payment/receipt to senior citizens.
21. Keep customers mailing list.
22. Send greeting cards on festivals.
23. Send special cards on promotion and achievements.
24. Attend to the customer needs.
25. Offer cold drinks/tea/coffee and biscuits.

26. Celebrate important festivals.
27. Attend functions arranged by customers.
28. Provide consultations on investments.
29. Keep the toilets (wash rooms) clean.
30. Walk with the customer to the exit to say good bye.

BIBLIOGRAPHY

THE MANAGEMENT BIBLE BY BOB NELSON & PETER ECONOMY INCREDIBLE CUSTOMER SERVICE BY DAVID FREEMANTLE THRIVING ON CHAOS BY TOM PETERS

SUCCESS IN COMMUNICATION BY STUART SILLARS HOW TO SUCCEED IN SELLING BY ALFRED TACK GETTING & DONE BY ROGER FISHER & ALAN SHARP WHY CRM DOESN'T WORK BY FREDERICK NEWELL REENGINEERING MANAGEMENT BY JAMES CHAMPY THE GOOD MANAGER'S GUIDE BY TREVOR BOUTALL FIRST THINGS FIRST BY STEPHEN R.COVEY

THE PURSUIT OF WOW BY TOM PETERS

IN-HOUSE TELE MARKETING BY THOMAS A. MCCAFFERTY

IN SEARCH OF EXCELLENCE BY TOM PETERS AND ROBERT H. WATERMAN JR NUTS BY KEVIN FREIBERG & JACKIE FREIBERG

SUCCESSFUL MANAGER'S HANDBOOK BY BRIAN L. DAVIS

LOWELL W. HELLERVIK, CAROL J. SKUBE, SUSAN H.GEBELEIN JAMES L. SHEARD.

PRINCIPLES OF MARKETING BY PHILIP KOTLER AND GARY ARMSTRONG. MARKETING MANAGEMENT BY PHILIP KOTLER.

Selling to win by Denny Richard.

Delighting your customers by Owton, Arvil.

Customer care by Sarah Cook.

Making meetings work by Will COCKS, GRAHAM.

www.ingramcontent.com/pod-product-compliance
Lightning Source LLC
Chambersburg PA
CBHW021943170526
45157CB00003B/908